D0713419

DATE DUE

THE ANGLO-SAXONS
HOW THEY LIVED AND WORKED

The Anglo-Saxons:

HOW THEY LIVED AND WORKED

G. A. Lester.

DAVID & CHARLES,
NEWTON ABBOT   LONDON   VANCOUVER
[Eng.]:

Distributed in U.S.A. by Dufour Editions Inc.

FOR AMY, NAN AND JACK

ISBN 0 7153 7248 3

Set in 11 on 12½pt Baskerville
and printed in Great Britain
by Redwood Burn Limited,
Trowbridge and Esher
for David & Charles (Publishers) Limited
Brunel House Newton Abbot Devon

Published in Canada
by Douglas David & Charles Limited
1875 Welch Street North Vancouver BC

Contents

Introduction

FOR this account of the society and working life of the Anglo-Saxons, a variety of sources has been drawn upon, in particular the studies of archaeology, placenames, ancient documents, literature and art.

The early documentary evidence, what little of it there is, comes from foreign writers, for the Anglo-Saxons themselves did not learn to write, or paint, on parchment until after the establishment of Christianity. Anglo-Saxon written and pictorial sources give much first-hand information about Christian times, but tend to be more concerned with religion and the higher strata of society than everyday matters or men and women of low rank. Placenames, on the other hand, though more restricted in the detail of the information they can give, relate to all periods of Anglo-Saxon England, alluding to many everyday activities, and are particularly useful in helping us to understand the earliest settlement.

A special word needs to be said about Anglo-Saxon archaeology, for in recent years the subject has developed with bewildering speed. Until about twenty-five years ago, almost all the material evidence concerning Anglo-Saxon daily life came either from chance discoveries of stray remains, or from the objects which the pagan Anglo-Saxons buried in the graves of their dead. Virtually nothing was known about their houses or the layout of their villages and towns, because the Anglo-Saxons used perishable building materials, such as timber and thatch, which rotted away in the course of time. Their dwelling-places are difficult to locate, excavate and interpret, so that in the past buildings were either missed or misinterpreted.

Nowadays the discovery of sites is greatly assisted by aerial photography, and by the fact that experienced archaeologists are becoming increasingly aware of what to look out for. Excavation is carried out by stripping the ground, layer by layer, over a large area until discolourations in the soil reveal the positions of post-holes and trenches. The interpretation of the intricate complex of features is a matter of difficulty, for houses were constantly being rebuilt, expanded and resited; and even when the groundplan of a building may be distinguished, the superstructure can never be reconstructed with certainty. However, as experience grows, the information yielded by buildings, and by the objects found in them, continues to enlarge our knowledge of Anglo-Saxon daily life at all periods.

Chronology

409	Following the withdrawal of the Romans as their Empire is threatened, the Britons are told to fend for themselves
c449	Hengist and Horsa invited to Britain as mercenaries (Bede)
c477	Ælle, founder of Sussex, lands near Selsey Bill (*Anglo-Saxon Chronicle*)
c495	Cerdic, founder of Wessex, lands in Hampshire (*Anglo-Saxon Chronicle*)
c500	Major British victory over the Anglo-Saxons at 'Mons Badonicus' (Gildas; date given by Bede as 493)
c545	A Welsh monk, Gildas, writes about the settlement of Britain
c555	Procopius states that Britain is inhabited by Britons, Angles, and Frisians
563	Columba, coming from Ireland, founds a Celtic monastery on Iona
597	Christianity introduced from Rome into Kent by Augustine
625	Paulinus, follower of Augustine, converts Edwin at York but is forced to leave when Edwin is killed in 632
635	Aidan travels from Iona to found a Celtic-style monastery on Lindisfarne as a centre for the conversion of the north
625-60	Rich ship-burial at Sutton Hoo, Suffolk
c650-c735	The golden age of Northumbrian art and learning

663   Synod of Whitby at which the customs of the Celtic Christians are superseded by the Roman ritual

731   Bede's *Ecclesiastical History* finished

757-96   Offa king of Mercia. Period of Mercian dominance

c789   First Viking raid mentioned in *Anglo-Saxon Chronicle*

793-4   Sack of monasteries at Lindisfarne and Jarrow by Vikings

850   Danish Vikings first spend the winter in England

871-99   Alfred king of Wessex

c886   Alfred, by treaty with Guthrum, agrees upon boundaries with the Danes. The area of Scandinavian settlement is later called the Danelaw

c891   Earliest surviving version of the *Anglo-Saxon Chronicle* begins

899-924   Edward the Elder king of Wessex. Beginning of reconquest of the Danelaw

924-939   Athelstan king of Wessex. Completion of reconquest

937   Major victory by Athelstan at *Brunanburh* (site not identified)

c950-1000   Revival of Benedictine monasticism under the influence of Dunstan, Æthelwold and Oswald

975-   Many books and works of art produced, especially at Winchester and Canterbury

978-1013   Æthelred 'the Unready' king of England

991   English defeat by Vikings at Maldon (Essex), later celebrated in an heroic poem

c1000   The four major extant books of Old English poetry written down

1014   Æthelred driven out by Swein, a Dane

1016-1035   Cnut, a Dane, king of England

1042-66   Edward the Confessor, son of Æthelred, king of England when Danish royal line ends

1066   Norman Conquest. End of Anglo-Saxon State

1

The Anglo-Saxons: Who They Were

THEIR NAME

THE Anglo-Saxons were of Germanic stock, settling in Britain after the withdrawal of the Romans at the beginning of the fifth century. This was not an organised migration, and the name 'Anglo-Saxon' had no relevance to any specific tribal group on the mainland of Europe. Their earliest settlements were based on small family or clan units, so that a general name for the whole people was not at first applicable and did not become current until the ninth century. Deriving from the Latin *Anglo-Saxonicus*, it was originally used to distinguish the English Saxons from the Old Saxons who remained on the Continent. Alfred the Great, himself Saxon, called his language *Englisc*, 'Angle-ish', and his people *Angel-cynn*, 'Angle-race', so it seems that the distinction between Angles and Saxons, even if initially important, did not remain significant.

THEIR ORIGIN

It is not certain where these people originated, but a good number of them came from northern Germany and the Danish peninsula. Tacitus, a Roman historian of the first century AD, has given in his *Germania* the first account of the Angles, whom he described as one of a confederation of tribes living near the coast who were distinguished by their worship of a fertility goddess, Nerthus. Later writers suggest

Fig 1 The location in England of Bede's 'Angles, Saxons and Jutes'

that their territory was bounded on the south by the river Eider. The Saxons are not mentioned by Tacitus, possibly because they were not a clearly defined group but a loose association of tribes. They were southern neighbours of the Angles and their territory extended west towards the marshlands of Frisia, now part of modern Holland. Some of the metalwork and pottery from Anglo-Saxon England closely resembles that found in these areas.

Unfortunately the origins of the first Englishmen are not as simple as this. The monk Bede of Jarrow, writing early in the eighth century, describes the newcomers as Angles, Saxons and Jutes, and says that the Jutes came from the area north of the Angles (present-day Denmark), and settled in Kent, the Isle of Wight and upon the mainland opposite. Archaeology does not fully support this, but rather emphasises the connection of these supposed Jutish people with the inhabitants of the Frankish Rhineland.

Another more nearly contemporary writer, Procopius of Caesarea, describes the inhabitants of sixth-century Britain as Britons, Angles and Frisians and, although no other early source supports him, his inclusion of the Frisians is borne out by archaeology, placenames and the close connection between English and Frisian – a language spoken in the Dutch province of Friesland, parts of Schleswig and on some of the neighbouring islands.

It is fruitless to search for too specific a homeland for the migrants, for it is likely that a mixture of tribes was involved in a general drift towards Britain. At this time there was great instability and movement among peoples throughout Europe, a general upheaval in which the north shared. This movement, beginning with the wanderings of the Goths in the third century, and ending with the settlement of the Vikings in the ninth, was intimately linked with the collapse of the Roman Empire. It was an heroic age, in which new kingdoms arose and old ones fell, and it thus provided much of the subject matter for Germanic epics and legends, including those of the Anglo-Saxons.

EARLIEST SETTLEMENTS

The earliest Germanic settlers were mercenaries employed by the Romans. Some were used to garrison the seaforts of the 'Saxon Shore' and were therefore deployed against their own compatriots who harried the eastern and southern coasts of Roman Britain in piratical bands. The presence of these mercenaries is known from Romano-Saxon pottery, in which Roman techniques are adapted to barbarian styles; from burials with grave goods, such as that of the fourth-century warrior at Richborough Castle in Kent; and from the remains of their huts inside the Roman towns and fortresses of the Saxon Shore, such as Porchester (Hampshire).

The main influx of the Anglo-Saxons came after the middle of the fifth century. The earliest written evidence of this is given by Gildas, a Welsh monk whose *Overthrow and Conquest of the Britons* is not so much an historical work as an attack upon the cowardice of the Britons after the Roman withdrawal in 409. Gildas says that an unnamed 'proud king' of Britain, following established Roman practice, invited the Saxons to help defend the country against the Picts and Scots. Three ships' companies of Saxons arrived and were given land in the eastern part of Britain. Later, after they had been joined by further forces, they revolted against their British employers, thus beginning that long struggle subsequently famous for its association with King Arthur. About the year 500, a decisive British victory at an unidentified place called 'Mons Badonicus' brought about a peace which was still unbroken at the time Gildas was writing (c 545).

The details of this tradition can be neither supported nor denied, for there are no other early written accounts, and archaeology and placenames give only a general idea of the earliest trends in settlement. From a distribution of cemeteries (assuming that this approximated to the pattern of their villages), it appears that the lands first taken were along the eastern and southern coasts, and that the settlers pushed inland by means of the rivers, particularly the Thames and those which drain into the Wash, and possibly the track through the Fens called the Icknield Way.

The most useful placenames are those like Hastings, 'Hæsta's people', and Reading, 'Reada's people', in which the element *-ingas* (plural of Old English *-ing*) is added to a personal name to denote the followers or dependants of a tribal leader. These are folknames which became attached to places when a group made its settlement, and therefore belong to an early period before the formation of the English kingdoms. Some names refer to the varied origin of the settlers, such as Swaffham (Norfolk), 'homestead or village of the Swabians', a tribe which once shared a border with the continental Angles at the river Eider, and Friston (Suffolk), Frieston (Lincs), 'farmstead or village of the Frisians'. The discovery of a royal ship-burial with strong Swedish connections at Sutton Hoo (Suffolk) has additionally emphasised the mixed character of the migrants to Britain.

SURVIVAL OF THE BRITONS

Placename study also helps to reveal the attitude of the Anglo-Saxons to the people they conquered. Many Britons withdrew into Cornwall, Wales and Strathclyde, or crossed the sea to Brittany, but name-borrowings from the Britons show that some remained in England and that the Anglo-Saxons learned to communicate with them. This contact increased as the English hold over the country was extended. The names borrowed were mainly those of natural features such as hills or rivers, but some folknames were taken over as well, for instance Kent, 'the land of the Cantii' and Cumberland, 'the land of the Cymry'. Few settlement names were carried over, for the English preferred new villages sited in accordance with their own demands for safety and comfort, but names of Roman towns and forts, many of which were Celtic in origin, often survive in Old English.

Celtic river names demonstrate increasing co-existence. In the first phase of settlement, east of a line drawn from Humberside to the Isle of Wight, these river names are confined to large and medium-sized rivers. Further west more Celtic names occur and include smaller rivers, hills and woods, while in the final stages of settlement in the north-west and west midlands, and south-west as far as Cornwall, the names of small streams and even villages are taken over. Names like Walton (Cheshire, Derbyshire) in which the first element is *walh* 'a Welshman, foreigner, serf', probably indicate the presence of small groups of Britons in Anglo-Saxon or Scandinavian areas. The small number of Celtic words absorbed into English include *bin* 'receptacle (originally of wickerwork)', *coomb* 'valley', and *tor* 'hill, rocky peak'. In the early eighth century, St Guthlac was troubled in his hermitage in the Fens by demons which he thought spoke British.

EARLY KINGDOMS

Gildas' account is elaborated by the Venerable Bede in his *Ecclesiastical History of the English People*, completed in 731. Unfortunately its authority as a description of the earliest settlement is lessened by its comparatively late date. Bede gives 449 as the year of the invitation to the Saxons, and names the British king, Vortigern, and the mercenary leaders, Hengist and Horsa. He then mentions the consolidated kingdoms of his own day:

> *From the Jutes are descended the people of Kent, and of the Isle of Wight, and also those in the province of the West Saxons who are to this day called Jutes, living opposite to the Isle of Wight. From the Saxons, that is, the country which is now called Old Saxony, came the East Saxons, the South Saxons and the West Saxons. From the Angles, that is, the country called Anglia, which is said since then to have remained deserted to this day, between the provinces of the Jutes and the Saxons, are descended the East Angles, the Middle Angles, the Mercians, all the race of the Northumbrians, that is, of those nations that live on the north side of the river Humber, and the other nations of the English.*

It is not possible from the archaeology of the pagan period to distinguish groups which correspond to these divisions.

However, the people of Kent, and to some extent the Isle of Wight, stand out as markedly the most prosperous, probably because of their advantageous trading position with the Continent. Their graves contain a relative abundance of gold and garnet jewellery, glassware, and sometimes enigmatic, perforated, silver spoons and polished rock-crystal balls set in silver bands, not found in other areas of England. Distinctive methods of landholding and class division are a further indication of their independence. The east-Anglian kingdom was rich and powerful by the seventh century and in the Sutton Hoo ship-burial we have the regalia and effects of one of its kings, breathtaking in their magnificence, and completely at odds with the common impression of the Anglo-Saxons as a nation of uncivilised farmers. Other archaeological distinctions also appear. A particular find in graves around the upper Thames and in Sussex is the so-called 'saucer' brooch, found also in the area of north Europe where the Saxons originated. In some Anglian areas, such as Cambridgeshire and Yorkshire, it was fashionable to wear gilded, bronze wristclasps sewn to the sleeve to fasten the cuff. A predominance of inhumations distinguishes Kent, Essex, Sussex and Wessex from East Anglia and Mercia, where the dead were normally cremated. In Middle Anglia a mixture of rites prevailed, while north of the Humber inhumation was again the main method of disposing of the dead. In short, archaeology suggests a complex situation which Bede may have simplified.

The compiler of the *Anglo-Saxon Chronicle*, a series of annals first put together towards the end of the ninth century, did indeed offer definite dates for the founding of some of the English kingdoms:

> *495 In this year two princes, Cerdic and Cynric his son, came to Britain with five ships at the place called* Cerdisesora *and the same day fought against the Britons . . .*
> *519 In this year Cerdic and Cynric obtained the kingdom.*

A later scribe has added 'and from that day on the princes of the West Saxons have reigned'. This type of dating is extremely doubtful since it often conflicts with the known facts, the *Chronicle* was probably instigated by King Alfred and reflects a strong West-Saxon point of view. For contemporary events it is of first importance, but for early events unreliable.

The fate of small tribes like the Hwicce of the Severn valley – whether they were engulfed by the expanding Mercians or West Saxons – is just not known, but their name survives in Whichford (Warwickshire) and Wychwood (Oxfordshire). The submergence of others, like the Middle Angles whom Bede was careful to distinguish, is equally poorly understood. The later history of the country is better documented and the picture which emerges is one of shifting power, sometimes modified by outside influences such as attack from abroad, with control over the whole country eventually being won by the West Saxons.

2

How They Lived

HOUSE AND HALL

AN account of the main types of building does well to begin with royal residences, and the logical starting point is at Yeavering (Northumberland), where a site, discovered and identified by a combination of aerial photography and documentary evidence, was excavated in 1953-7. Yeavering was a country residence of the kings of Northumbria, the sort of establishment to which the court progressed for a time in order to live off the produce of various scattered estates in turn. Present-day names such as Kingston, Coniston, and Conisbrough reveal the widespread existence of these royal vills.

It was at Yeavering in 627, Bede tells us, that Paulinus preached Christianity and baptised the converted in the

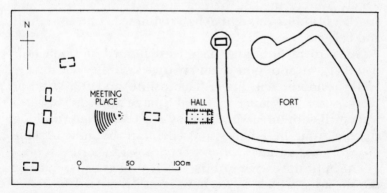

Fig 2   Yeavering royal palace. Plan of buildings in the time of King Edwin (616-32)

nearby river Glen. The buildings were all of timber, the most important being the great hall, dating originally from around 600, but rebuilt three times within the century. In the time of King Edwin (616-32) it was bout 90ft (27m) long internally, divided by aisle-posts and by a partition which formed a room at one end. There were also doors in the middle of each side. Westwards lay a scatter of smaller buildings, and to the east a large timber fort, for refuge in time of attack. An unexpected feature was a large timber grandstand, like a segment of a Roman theatre, which provided an assembly place. The buildings were destroyed by fire and rebuilt several times before the site was finally abandoned in favour of a new one about two miles away.

Another royal residence which has been excavated at Cheddar (Somerset) was in use from the ninth century until the fourteenth. In the time of King Alfred (871-99) it comprised a hall and various subsidiary buildings, the largest of these being perhaps a bower or private chamber for the king or his chief estate official, the reeve. The hall was bow-sided with two doors set at the sides, and measured 76 by 18ft (23 by 5.5m) internally. The squared posts of the walls were set close in pairs, suggesting the possibility of an upper storey. By the following century, when the king's *witan* (council) met at Cheddar, the palace had been rebuilt on a grander scale. There was a new hall, rectangular in shape, a chapel which overlay the old hall, a latrine, a new bower, and another building thought to be a combined grain store, mill and bakery.

Other royal buildings have been located at Doon Hill (Dunbar), Stratford-on-Avon (Warwickshire), Westminster Hall (London), Winchester (Hampshire) and Old Windsor (Berkshire). The latter included a large and sophisticated watermill with three wheels fed by a three-quarter-mile long channel from the Thames, and a domestic building of stone probably with glazed windows and possibly a tiled roof.

The opposite extreme of the social scale is represented by the pit-huts, which so far have been discovered in over a hundred villages. These were the earliest domestic buildings to be discovered and for many years gave the impression of an extremely low standard of living among the Anglo-Saxons. When a village of these huts was discovered at Sutton Courtenay (Oxfordshire) in 1921, the excavator was forced by their squalor and meanness to conclude that 'the bulk of the people, we can now be assured, were content with something that hardly deserves a better title than that of a hovel', a conclusion strangely at odds with the way of life described in Anglo-Saxon poetry and with the standards of luxury suggested by many of the excavated artefacts. It is now known that although these pit-huts were common they are by no means typical of Anglo-Saxon houses; sometimes they may be simply worksheds or stores associated with larger buildings.

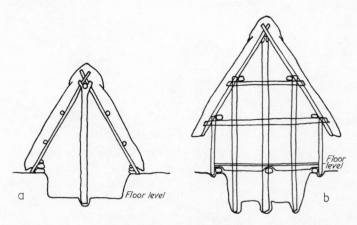

Fig 3   Two reconstructions of pit-huts: (a) Weald and Downland Museum; (b) West Stow

A reconstruction of a hut of this type at the Weald and Downland Open Air Museum in Sussex, based on two excavated examples, shows that the accommodation could be quite roomy. One of the originals, which was fairly typical, had a pit 12ft by 9ft by about 2ft (3.6m by 2.7m by 60cm) deep, two post-holes within the pit, for uprights to support a ridge, and a central hearth. In the reconstruction the rafters slope down to topsoil level where they are packed with rubble, and the gable ends are filled with wattle and daub.

Differing information comes from the village of West Stow (Suffolk), where burnt timber found in a hut with a sunken base shows that in this instance the building had a wooden floor, vertical plank walls and a thatched roof. This was only a weaving shed, a fact clearly shown by the presence of nearly 100 loom weights – annular clay rings which hung from the warp threads of an upright loom. The West Stow site is being made into a park containing reconstructions of the buildings. In the first one attempted, the pit has been interpreted as a cellar or airspace. The plank floor overlaps the edges of the pit and gives a total living area as large as 16 by 20ft (5 by 6m). Pit-huts survive from all periods, sometimes in large communities as at Mucking (Essex) where 132 had been reported by 1975.

Fig 4 Hypothetical reconstruction of hall at Chalton *(R. Warmington, Medieval Archaeology, XVI)*

Buildings of intermediate status, suitable as dwellings for free peasants, have recently been found in increasing numbers. In early Saxon villages such as West Stow and Chalton (Hampshire), rectangular, surface-built halls of modest size have been unearthed. One at West Stow, constructed upon single uprights set a foot deep (0.3m), measured 27 by 14ft (8.2 by 4.2m). A second, which measured 33 by 15ft (10 by 4.5m), had a central hearth, a partition at one end and shallow, double post-holes. In two slightly larger buildings at Chalton, a partitioned area at one end was further divided into three smaller rooms. The eight or so excavated at Maxey (Cambridgeshire) varied in length from 34 to 50ft (10.5-15.2m) and in width from 16 to 22ft (4.8-6.6m); they were constructed with posts variously set in individual holes, in continuous trenches, or on wooden groundsills. In one, the central groundsill shows that the interior was divided lengthways by a row of upright posts, perhaps supporting a loft. A fragment of daub which was found suggests that wattle and daub was used for the walls. One of the buildings had a large double door reminiscent of a barn, but finds of pottery, loom weights, whetstones, querns, knives, pins, shears, an arrowhead, combs and bones are clear proof of occupation.

The clearest example of a nobleman's residence is a group of buildings at Sulgrave (Northamptonshire). The main one was a hall over 82ft (25m) long with a cobbled porch and screened-off service area. It had a central hearth and apparently benches along one side. Projecting at right-angles, making the building L-shaped, was a chamber-block which had stone footings which still survive to a height of about 3¼ft (1m). This part seems to have had an upper storey. Subsidiary buildings included a gatehouse and a kitchen. The gatehouse also had walls partly of stone, in this case still standing to a height of 7ft (2.1m).

Other types of evidence for Anglo-Saxon buildings can be briefly mentioned. The Bayeux Tapestry, probably designed by an Englishman soon after the Norman Conquest, shows a number of houses and helps to suggest their construction methods and details. Ten halls are depicted. One has an upper floor reached by an outside stair. Others have a projection on the roof, possibly a louvre by which smoke might find its way out from a hearth in the middle of the floor. There are five illustrations of Edward the Confessor's hall at Westminster, showing it to have been an aisled, single-storey building with corner turrets. Two town houses are shown, both with upper rooms and one with a balcony, and there are three simple cottages with walls horizontally planked or tile-hung, all without windows. Roofs are of tile, shingle, or thatch.

Sculptured tombstones are another possible source of information for they are sometimes in the form of houses shaped like upturned boats and may provide evidence concerning the superstructure of halls with bowed sides, such as the early one at Cheddar.

Literature is also helpful. The author of *Beowulf* probably drew upon his knowledge of hall life in describing the great royal residence which the troll, Grendel, terrorised. This had a paved or perhaps a wooden, polished floor, timber walls strengthened with iron clamps, decorated gables, tapestries, an open hearth and benches which were cleared before bedding and pillows were spread out.

A late tenth-century prose writer named Byrhtferth is also incidentally helpful when, in his *Manual*, he compares the process of learning to a carpenter preparing to build: 'First of all he surveys the site of the house, and cuts the timber, and neatly fits together the sills, and lays down the beams, and fastens the rafters to the roof-ridge, and supports it with buttresses, and afterwards he pleasantly decorates the house.'

Several entries in the *Anglo-Saxon Chronicle* are of some use, that for 978 providing additional evidence of two-storey buildings: 'In this year the leading councillors of England fell down from an upper room at Calne, all except the holy archbishop Dunstan, who remained alone standing on a beam.' The use of stone for royal buildings is mentioned by Asser, biographer of King Alfred, who wrote of 'the royal halls and chambers wonderfully built of stone and wood at his command'.

Finally, there are the wills, particularly those of women, which provide a little information about the house furnishings of the wealthy. That of Wynflæd in the tenth century mentions 'two chests and in them her best bed curtain and a linen covering and all the bed-clothing which goes with it . . . a long hall tapestry and a short one and three seat coverings . . . and a little spinning box'.

VILLAGES

Most Anglo-Saxons lived in villages or upon the estates of the wealthy. Early patterns of settlement are not yet understood in any detail. They would vary from one district to the next, but it is clear from the distribution of pagan cemeteries that the Anglo-Saxons made much use of water transport and sited their earliest homes near navigable waters, by means of which they penetrated far inland. A distribution map of the upper Thames valley, for instance, shows burial places clustering around the rivers Cherwell, Evenlode, Windrush and the Thames itself, in far greater numbers than around the Roman roadways. The settlers naturally preferred sites with good amenities such as fresh water, shelter, defence and fertile, well drained soil, but one must bear in mind that conditions affecting the first settlements may no longer have applied after the more obvious sites had been taken. In the sixth and seventh centuries the Anglo-Saxons pushed into marginal areas like West Yorkshire where they ousted the Britons from their still-independent kingdom of Elmet. Some villages were established on dry ground amongst marshes, as is shown by names like Romsey (Hampshire) and Battersea (London) which originate in part from Old English *eg* 'island', 'dry ground in a fen'. Other villages, such as the group at Chalton, were established, for some reason, on exposed downland, while the site of the early and perhaps military settlement at Mucking was probably dictated by its strategic position overlooking the Thames estuary.

Some of the excavated settlements help to suggest the layout of rural villages and country residences. The royal vills of Yeavering and Cheddar point to the central importance of the hall, the apparent lack of rigidly planned layout, the provision necessary for defence; Maxey demonstrates the grouping of halls around an unoccupied central area; an episcopal estate at North Elmham (Norfolk) shows division of the site into rectangles by means of boundary ditches. West Stow is at present the most fully investigated early village. Six halls have been found here and sixty-eight sunken huts, some of which were loosely grouped around the halls. There were also temporary animal pens, boundary ditches and evidence of home industry, notably weaving and bone-working.

TOWNS

Town life seems to have been disliked by most Anglo-Saxons until the time when Viking raids and an increasingly mercantile economy made urban living more desirable. In any case, most towns were no larger than many present-day villages, and the animals, farmland and agricultural buildings attached to them must have presented a very rural appearance.

A distinction needs to be made between old towns, used by the Romans and taken over by the Anglo-Saxons, and new towns which grew up as market centres or strongholds. The extent to which Roman towns continued, or were later reoc-cupied, is not known, but some remained inhabited because of their important geographical positions – such as Canter-bury, where the network of Roman roads converged, or York, which controlled the route from the north between the Pennines and the marshes of the Humber. The earliest Anglo-Saxon buildings known from Roman towns are of pit-hut type and there is no clear evidence of the use of stone until the coming of Christianity. According to Bede, Æthelbert's queen, Bertha, used to pray in the old stone church of St Martin in Canterbury, which had been built by British Christians in Roman times, and it was here that St Augustine first worshipped until he was allowed to build or repair churches in other places. Many Roman towns even‑tually became derelict, like Verulamium, the ruins of which were given to the monks of St Albans in the eighth century by Offa, and Chester, which is specifically described as deserted when the Danes occupied it while on the run from Alfred in 893.

Villages conveniently sited at the junction of important routes, at fords, harbours or near important estates, sometimes grew into new towns. It was in the interest of these communities to provide themselves with defences against attack, and in this way the fortified boroughs came into being. It was these strongholds that Alfred and his successors used as the basis of their *burh* (fort) system, strengthening existing defences and establishing others in hitherto unimportant places where the new security often attracted a population of craftsmen and traders. Old Roman defences were strengthened and repaired at Winchester and Exeter; natural features were made use of at Lydford (Devon) where the borough is situated on a hill spur; Wareham (Dorset) was fortified by a system of banks and ditches on a neck of land between two rivers, at a point where they flowed close together; South Cadbury (Somerset) made use of an ancient hillfort.

The best example of a late-Saxon town is Thetford (Norfolk), which, in the tenth and eleventh centuries, grew rich on river traffic becoming one of the largest towns in the kingdom and, between 1072 and 1094, the seat of the bishop of East Anglia. Apart from a few early pit-huts, the excavated buildings were mostly timber rectangles, the longest of which was a great aisled hall over 37yd (33m) long. Some had cellars with cobbled or mortared floors. There was a system of boundary ditches, arterial metalled and minor roads and some deliberate zoning of occupation – one area had the appearance of an industrial slum, and in another the larger buildings were concentrated. Near the town defences was a kilnyard in which a succession of kilns produced the characteristic wheel-turned Thetford ware. The accumulation of rubbish in two hundred years of occupation was less than might have been expected, which suggests that there may have been an organised system of refuse disposal. It is possible that even the abandonment of the old town in the eleventh century, in favour of a new site on the opposite bank of the river Ouse, was a centrally planned development, like the reoccupation of the old site by a housing estate in recent years.

Excavations at Lydford show that this small, remote, Devon town was also formally laid out in building plots relating to a street grid and to the earth and timber town wall. One property had a frontage of 80ft (24m) on the main street with the house set back 10ft (3m) from the road – more spacious than most houses in larger towns where property and land commanded higher prices. That town land became very expensive is shown by the fact that the community of the Old Minster at Winchester gave up a country estate of twelve hides (enough in theory for twelve families) in return for only two acres against the walls in their own town. Landowners throughout the country often bought property in towns, initially for use in transacting business and later as a property investment.

Some idea of the population of towns at the time of the Norman Conquest can be gathered from the Domesday survey. The Domesday Book is concerned not with exact population figures but with the number of burgesses in each town. Assuming an average of five persons per family, the figures would be approximately 8,000 for York, 5,000 for Lincoln and Norwich, 4,000 for Thetford, 3,500 for Oxford; sixteen others have estimated populations of 500 or more. For some large centres, such as London, Winchester and Bristol, no figures are given, but an estimated one and a half million population for the whole country seems a reasonable guess.

FOOD

The provision and storing of food must have been a constant problem for the early Anglo-Saxons. Hunting, fishing, gathering wild fruits and perhaps plunder were probably the earliest sources of supply until domesticated stock could be reared and the wasteland brought into cultivation. Beyond a little food deposited in graves as provision for the dead – nuts, some eggs and a little meat – no direct evidence is available about the eating habits of the earliest English. Presumably crops of wheat, barley, oats and rye were grown, for we find them mentioned in names such as Wheathill (Somerset), the numerous Bartons, 'barley', Haverhill (Suffolk) 'oats', and Ryhill (W Yorkshire). Placenames also refer to vegetables, such as beans at Banham (Norfolk), peas at

Peasenhall (Suffolk), cabbage at Colworth (Bedfordshire), and to fruits such as apples at Appledore (Kent), pears at Parbold (Lancashire), and plums at Plumstead (London). Names referring to domestic animals are particularly common, sometimes compounded with the element *wic*, 'dwelling-place, place where food is prepared, dairy farm'. Butterwick (Lincolnshire) and Cheswick (Northumberland) specifically mention foods which were processed there.

More information about foodstuffs in later times comes from documents, like one called *The Rights of Various People* which lists the customary dues received by workers on an estate. One hundred cheeses were the annual allowance of the cheesemaker, who was to make butter at her lord's table out of the whey pressed from the cheese; milk and whey for the herdsmen; twelve pounds of good corn, the carcasses of two sheep and one good cow as food for a male slave (less for a female). It was a perquisite of the granarykeeper to have all the corn spilled at the barn door at harvest time. The same document mentions the beekeeper who provided the honey necessary for mead and for sweetening food. His office is recorded in names like Bickerton (N Yorkshire). *The Rule of St Benedict*, observed widely in English monasteries from the tenth century, recommends for each day: two cooked meals, young vegetables and fruit as available, one pound of bread, and one pint of wine or more, 'care being taken in all things that excess and drunkenness do not creep in'. A novice monk's diet is given in   lfric's *Colloquy* (c 1000 AD) as meat, vegetables, eggs, fish, cheese, butter, beans, ale and water.

Preparation of food depended above all on the use of salt, for the Anglo-Saxons relied on salted provisions for a large part of the year. Salt was obtained by evaporating brine from seawater or inland springs, for rock salt was not worked in England until the seventeenth century. Saltmaking establishments, and the associated woodland which provided their fuel, are sometimes mentioned in charters. According to the Domesday Book, Norfolk had 64 villages owning up to 45 saltpans each, Lincolnshire and Sussex 34, with as many as 100 pans concentrated at Rye. The great centres of inland salt production were Cheshire and Worcestershire. In these counties, Middlewich, Nantwich, Northwich and particularly Droitwich, once the main salt town of England with 160 pans, demonstrate a specialised meaning of *wic*, 'a place where salt is prepared'.

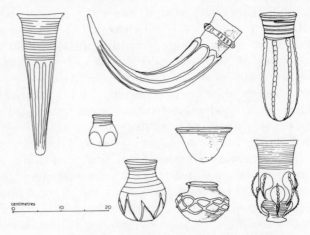

Fig 5   Glass vessels from pre-Christian graves

Some of the vessels and utensils used in the preparation and service of food have survived. In addition to the pottery described in the next chapter, there were vessels of leather, wood and metal; drinking horns such as the magnificent decorated pair from Taplow (Buckinghamshire); decorated cylindrical buckets constructed of wooden staves bound by bronze hoops; and a variety of fine, coloured glassware in the shape of beakers, jars, bottles, horns, bowls and palm cups – round-bottomed tumblers which spilled their contents if set down.

Although many simple iron knives have survived, some of which could have served for domestic use, we must rely on a small number of illustrations for an idea of cooking, serving and eating habits. The Bayeux Tapestry, which depicts William feasting at Hastings, shows a large suspended cookingpot, a rack of spitted fowls, and a baker using a pair of tongs to take bread or cakes off a stove and place them on a trencher. Servants or waiters arrange the food in dishes on a sidetable made of shields laid on trestles, and one of them blows a horn to announce that dinner is served. Amongst the dishes the only implements are knives. An old man is about to drink from his bowl and (rudely, we would think) is sprawling his elbow in front of Duke William.

HEALTH

Toilet objects from Anglo-Saxon graves show that men and women groomed themselves with bone combs, small shears, bronze tweezers, pickers and a variety of other gadgets. Some evidence for their physique and the general state of their health can be gathered from the condition of skeletal remains, most of which are from graves of the pagan period. The average height of men was about 5ft 6in (171cm) and of women about 5ft (156cm), a little less than in present-day England. Analysis of one group showed that over half (57.4 per cent) did not reach the age of thirty; of the remainder, 81.8 per cent were dead by the age of forty, and 97.5 per cent by fifty. Of the various degenerative conditions, by far the most common was osteoarthritis, especially of the lumbar region. A 'squatting facet' which sometimes developed at the ankle joints is said to indicate that the subjects were unused to stools and chairs, or that they did a great deal of work in a crouching position. Almost 20 per cent of the population had suffered fractures of some kind. The high incidence of fractures of the lower leg and wrist perhaps resulted from heavy agricultural labours. On the other hand, teeth are generally free from caries, though often worn down by mastication of coarse food.

Documentary sources describe in dramatic terms the plagues and famines which swept across the country. In 686, for example, a pestilence carried off almost all the brotherhood of the monasteries of Monkwearmouth and Jarrow, Bede being one of the few to survive. In the centuries which followed, the frequent epidemics were aggravated by the Viking wars. The *Anglo-Saxon Chronicle* records graphically how one hardship upon another debilitated and demoralised the people, even in the reign of the last Saxon king, Edward the Confessor. In 1042 the weather was severe, and 'more cattle died than anyone remembered before, either from disease or because of the harsh weather'. In 1044 'there was a very great famine, and corn was dearer than anyone remembered'. In 1047 another severe winter caused mortality of men and cattle, and 'both birds and fish died because of the hard frost and from hunger'. A further outbreak in 1048 was accompanied by earthquakes and wildfire. Times must have been hard.

Surviving medical books, treatises and charms give more specific information about diseases and their treatment. There are prescriptions for headache ('broken head'), vertigo, failing sight, eyesores, earache, deafness, toothache, swellings on the body, shortness of breath, coughs, hiccups, jaundice, digestive afflictions, urinary diseases, falling hair, fever, gout, dropsy, dysentery, miscarriages, haemorrhoids, insomnia, paralysis, fits, rabies, a whole range of skin complaints and a variety of conditions not identified with any certainty. The methods of treatment were mainly magical (see Chapter 5) and herbal. For instance,

> *to make a pleasant drink against the devil and insanity, put into ale some hassock, lupine, carrot, fennel, radish, betony, water-agrimony, marche, rue, wormwood, cat's mint, elecampane, enchanter's nightshade and teazle. Sing twelve masses over the potion and let the patient drink it. He will soon be better.*

Bathing was recommended, although we read that ascetics like St Etheldreda rarely availed themselves of this luxury. Steam baths were produced by pouring water over heated stones. To keep a sick man warm it was considered helpful 'that a fat child sleep with him'. Some surgery was undertaken, including amputation of gangrenous limbs, abdominal surgery for hernia, 'should a man's bowels prolapse', and the following procedure for a hare lip: 'Cut with a knife and sew tight with a silk thread; then smear the [prescribed] salve inside and out before the silk rots. If it puckers, smooth out with the hand'. Blood-letting and cauterisation were also practised, but not always in the part of the body which was afflicted.

DRESS AND FASHION

Although the pre-Christian dead who were not cremated were usually buried in full dress, the materials have decayed to such an extent that little can now be deduced from them about the style and shape of early Anglo-Saxon garments. The small pieces of fabric which are sometimes found suggest that the commonest materials were wool and linen. In the chieftain's barrow-burial at Taplow, two woollen braids made by tablet-weaving had been embellished by a brocade of golden threads less than half a millimetre thick. The original patterns are recoverable from the faint impression of the weave upon the gold. The twenty or so other examples of this technique in England are all from women's graves dating from the sixth century and give an idea of the rich headbands, frontals, and woven bracelets in vogue amongst the wealthy. Apart from this, there is only the evidence of fastenings, such as brooches, buckles, strap-ends

Fig 6   Typical male and female costume

and wristclasps, to indicate prevailing fashions.

There is more evidence for later Anglo-Saxon times. Pictures in manuscripts – when due allowance has been made for their stylisation – are useful if they show scenes based on everyday life. The Bayeux Tapestry and some carvings are informative. So too are documents like the will of Wynflæd (p 24), which refers to her 'double badger-skin [?] gown, and another of linen . . . and her best dun tunic, and the better of her cloaks . . . her black tunics and her best holy veil . . . and her best headband . . . and her cap'. Piecing all this evidence together we have a picture of the rich lady with her full length, tight-sleeved tunic, loose gown hitched up with matching girdle, cloak, fastened perhaps with a brooch at the neck, and flowing veil enveloping her shoulders but exposing her face. Her husband might wear a knee-length tunic with tight, puckered sleeves and a short cloak fastened with a brooch at the shoulder so as to leave his swordarm free. In an older man, the garments would be more enveloping and flowing. Legwear consisted of breeches, hose, socks or legbandages, with shoes or boots. Men frequently wore small leather caps and, like the women, kept their hair quite long. On the Bayeux Tapestry longer hair and moustaches distinguish the English from the Normans, who are sometimes shaved from the nape almost to the crown of the head. The poor wore fewer and coarser garments. For instance, most of the workers depicted in the Anglo-Saxon calendar (p 49) wear only a short tunic and go barefoot even in December and January.

The jewellery with which clothes were held together and adorned is well demonstrated by many surviving examples. Brooches are particularly numerous, and were worn by both men and women to secure the hood and the gown. There are three main types. Cast bronze longbrooches were the most popular. These had a bow, into which the cloth was gathered, a flat head, a narrow foot and a pin at the back. Two common varieties are 'cruciform' and 'square-headed'. Ringbrooches were either 'annular' or 'penannular' (complete or broken ring). In this type the cloth of the garment was pushed upwards through the ring and secured by a

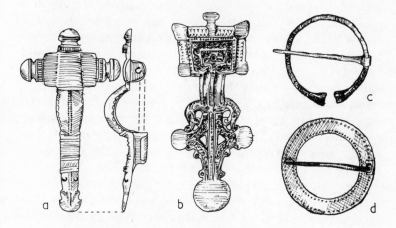

Fig 7   Longbrooches and ringbrooches: (a) cruciform; (b) square-
headed; (c) penannular; (d) annular

Fig 8   Design on the silver Fuller Brooch – diameter 4½in

hinged or separate pin. Solid roundbrooches are the third type, and consist of an ornamental disc with a pin and catch on the back. Saxon 'saucer' brooches belong to this category as do the most elaborate of all, the so-called 'jewelled round-brooches', most common in Kent in pre-Christian times. These were made of gold or silver with garnets and lapis lazuli set in *cloisons* (cells), arranged in the shapes of stars or concentric circles. Larger, regularly spaced garnets were sometimes raised up on bosses of shell or ivory, interspersed with panels of gold filigree. The brooch from Kingston in Kent (p 67) is the finest example of this type.

Fewer brooches are found dating from Christian times because they were no longer buried in graves. It seems that gold was very rarely used, probably because of shortage of supply, so that silver became more popular. Several large, silver disc-brooches survive from the ninth century, their faces ornamented with carved designs accentuated by inlays of a black substance called *niello*. The increasing variety of design subjects was due to the influence of Scandinavian and classical art. For example, the Fuller Brooch in the British Museum probably depicts personifications of the five senses, sight (centre) and (clockwise) smell, feeling, hearing and taste.

The finest necklace surviving (now in the British Museum) is that of a rich lady from Desborough (Northamptonshire), and consists of 8 cabochon garnets, 9 plain gold drops and 19 gold spacing-pieces with a pendant Latin cross. Less wealthy women adorned themselves with beads of glass, amber, amethyst, rock-crystal and a variety of other materials, which they sometimes hung in strings or festoons on the head, breast or from the waist. Sometimes they wore cruciform or circular pendants, like the gold filigree cross from Winster (Derbyshire), or the garnet and gold pendant from Wilton (Norfolk) which is built up around a golden *solidus* of the Byzantine emperor Heraclitus (AD 410-41).

Other trinkets include pins of metal and bone for the hair, headdress and breast. On the breast, they might be worn in suites of two or even three pins linked by a chain. A pair of seventh-century gold pins, 2in (5cm) long, with garnet-set heads linked by a gold chain, comes from a mound at Cowlow (Derbyshire), and a set of three, in silvergilt, was found in the river Witham at Fiskerton (Lincolnshire). The largest pin is about 5in (13cm), and all three have large circular heads with interlaced, dragon-like animals. Simple earrings, of pierced-ear type, were worn. So too were simple finger rings of metal, bone and ivory. A small number have indecipherable inscriptions in the ancient characters known as runes, and there are two royal rings, inscribed with the names of King Æthelwulf (836-67) and Queen Æthelswith (855-89).

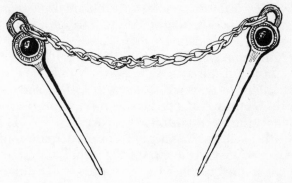

Fig 9 Gold and garnet pin-suite from Cowlow – pin length 2in

Finally buckles, clasps and strap-mounts must be mentioned, as these are among the most skilful examples of the jeweller's art. Those from the ship-burial at Sutton Hoo were probably items of royal regalia. They include golden buckles, hinges, clasps, ornamental studs and mounts, distributors and strap-ends, which adorned the royal harness (see p 145). But whether they belonged to the rich or the moderately well off, the essential features of Anglo-Saxon strap decoration are the same – they were functional items upon which the flat surfaces gave good opportunity to the craftsman to fill his subject with the riot of lively decoration which is the hallmark of his craft.

ENTERTAINMENT

We know a little about the activities with which the Anglo-Saxons amused themselves and absorbed their energies, but the full range and inventiveness of their sports and pastimes can only be guessed at.

Hunting and falconry, a means of livelihood for some, were considered fitting entertainment for others, and the interest which noblemen took in these pursuits is clearly shown in their bequests of horses, hunting-hounds and trained hawks. These were occupations fit for a king, and sometimes great efforts were made to obtain the best animals, as when Æthelbert the eighth-century king of Kent sent to Germany for two falcons which had been trained to kill cranes. On the Bayeux Tapestry the noble status of Harold and the peaceful purpose of his journey to France are both symbolised by the dogs which accompany him and the hawk which sits on his wrist. The law prohibited hunting on Sunday, and the penitentials of Archbishop Theodore specifically excluded the clergy from participation in it under any circumstances, prescribing one to three years' penance for any cleric who so indulged. Ordinary men probably enjoyed lowlier forms of field sport. The borders of the Bayeux Tapestry show what appears to be a wolf-hunt by men armed with clubs, and a man with a sling casting a stone at a bird in flight. Bear-baiting and bull-baiting were carried on, as well as trials of strength and athletics, swimming, horseracing and weapon sports such as archery, which sharpened a man's skills for war. Placenames such as Plaistow (Derbyshire) record Old English *pleg-stow*, 'a sports place, a place where people gathered for play'.

As for music making, it is clear that the Anglo-Saxons knew of the horn, trumpet, harp, lyre, pipe, shawm and rebec, for they depict them all in their manuscripts. A silver-plated trumpet is referred to in the will of Prince Æthelstan, and some Anglo-Saxon riddles also refer to musical instruments such as the reed-pipe and an enigmatic creature which sits at the feast with its nose hanging downwards and has bird-like feet and hands, in one of which there is a

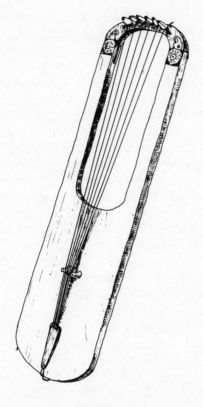

Fig 10 Reconstructed round-lyre from Sutton Hoo – length 29¼in

beautiful voice – probably bagpipes. The only instrument of which fragments have survived is the lyre. The remains of three are known from graves. The earliest, dating from the fifth century, is from Abingdon (Oxfordshire), the surviving pieces being the bone facings of the peg arm. The remains of two seventh-century lyres have been recovered from the aristocratic barrow-burials at Taplow and Sutton Hoo. The Sutton Hoo instrument has been recently reconstructed as a 'round-lyre', 29¼in long and 8¼in wide (74 by 21cm) with sound box and frame of maplewood and pegs of poplar (they could have been willow). It has six equal-length strings of gut (although the original strings might equally well have been of horsehair). The original bridge was lost, but would probably have been made of amber or bone. Manuscript pictures show that it would have been played on the knee. The instrument most often mentioned in Old English poetry is the harp. In *Beowulf* the brooding jealousy of the troll, Grendel, was aroused when he heard 'loud merriment in the hall, the music of the harp and the clear sound of the minstrel'. Grendel soon put a stop to that, but when Beowulf eventually defeated him, once again 'the joyful harp was struck, many a lay recited, when to bring joy to the hall King Hrothgar's minstrel sang among the meadbenches'. The harp was played and enjoyed by both clerics and laymen. Bede says that at Whitby Abbey (N Yorkshire) it was the custom to pass round a harp after a feast so that those present might entertain each other.

The Anglo-Saxons enjoyed eating and drinking together. An impression of this can be gained from food-rents and dues, drinking and eating vessels, halls, servants and the occasional historical record of feasts and banquets. But it is poetry which deals most graphically and fully with the subject. In *Beowulf* the men seat themselves in the royal hall on the benches according to rank, with the king in the centre near the hearth. We are told less about the food than about the drink – mead, ale and wine – which is brought around by cupbearers and the queen herself. The formal side of feasting is emphasised in the giving of gifts, the strict order of precedence and the public boasts and professions of loyalty. On the field of battle the warriors reminded each other of these brave boasts and taunted each other with the infamy of desertion. Ælfwine at the battle of Maldon encouraged his fellows: 'Remember the speeches which we often made at mead-drinking, when we warriors on the hall benches uttered our boasts about fierce battle. Now we can get to know who is brave.'

But this was aristocratic life; we know much less about the habits of ordinary people. Pre-Christian festivals were probably times of great indulgence, for the church was anxious to substitute 'religious feasting' for the sacrifice of oxen which had formerly taken place and which was a tradition too entrenched to be done away with. Relatives and friends sometimes feasted and drank at the dead man's wake. *The*

Rights of Various People tells us that workers customarily received a harvest feast for reaping the corn and a drinking feast for ploughing. Despite the lack of substantial information, we can be sure that the working people knew how to enjoy themselves in times of plenty as well as their masters.

Some indoor games survive, although, unfortunately, we do not know the rules. Hemispherical, bone playingpieces or counters, probably for use in a game akin to draughts, are sometimes found in burials. At New Inns (Derbyshire) a set of twenty-eight was found, most with 8, 9, or 10 incised dots on the convex surface. Elsewhere sets of up to fifty such pieces have come to light. Perhaps they were used in the game called *tæfl* which is mentioned in Old English poetry. There is also mention of a coloured or chequered board, but no example remains. Sets of sheep's ankle-bones which are sometimes found could belong to another game. At least thirty-one were recovered from a cremation urn at Caistor-by-Norwich (Norfolk), the largest of which has an indecipherable runic inscription. Another possibility is that they were used in lot-casting.

Word games were certainly popular, particularly riddles, and a collection of ninety-four has been preserved in Old English verse, with many more in Latin. These are not so much riddles in the modern sense as enigmatic descriptions, often spoken by the object in question, which are at once both accurate and misleading. Here is an example:

> *I saw the creature in question with its greatly swollen belly on its back. A servant came behind, a very strong man, who had suffered a great deal when its fullness of wind flew out through its eye. It does not always die when it must give up what is inside it, but revival comes once again into its bosom, and its breath [or prosperity, a play on words] is restored. It begets a son which is its own father.*

The answer is 'bellows'. These riddles range from the learned and verbal to the suggestive and indecent. There is even a humourous catch-riddle:

A creature came along where many wise men were sit-ting at an assembly. It had one eye and two ears and two feet, twelve hundred heads, a back and a belly and two hands, arms and shoulders, one neck and two sides. Say what I am called.

Answer (apparently): 'a one-eyed onion-seller'.

3

How They Worked

THE FARMING YEAR

A SHORT treatise of the eleventh century called *The Wise Reeve* lists the qualities and abilities of the ideal steward of an estate. He is to supervise all things of whatever importance 'in town and down, in wood and on water, in field and fold, both within and without'. In particular, it mentions the chief occupations of the farming year, starting with summer.

In May, June and July he must see that the labourers harrow, cart dung to the fields, make sheepfolds and hurdles, shear sheep, build and repair, erect fences, fetch timber, dig up weeds, and make fishing weirs and mills. During August, September and October he must organise the harvest, reap, mow and bring home the various crops. At this time he must also direct thatching, roofing, cleaning of oxfolds, repair of shippons and sheep-pens, and then begin the ploughing before the frosts. In winter he must see that sufficient timber is cut and that orchards are planted, and attend to various jobs such as threshing, woodchopping, making cattle-stalls and pigsties, fowl-perches, ovens and corn-drying kilns in the yard. In spring he must again oversee the ploughing, set vineyards and graft new shoots, dig, cut the park hedge, and soon after that, if the weather holds, sow beans, linseed and woadseed, set madder and plant the vegetable patch. He had a lot to do.

Pictures of the year's labours, month by month, in an Anglo-Saxon calendar (Plate 1), also of the eleventh century, give further illustration of the various agricultural duties. It would be unwise to place too much emphasis on the conven-

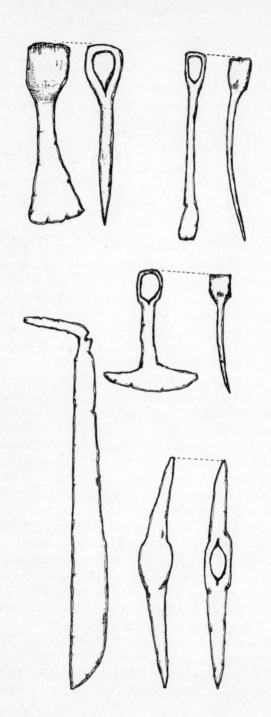

Fig 11 Tools from Hurbuck

tionalised sequence of the occupations, but there are many features which are part of a specifically English calendar tradition. The year begins with ploughing in January, and proceeds through pruning of fruit trees and vines to pickaxing, digging and raking in March. Seed is sown at this time, as well as in January. April shows three seated figures drinking, perhaps to celebrate the end of the Lenten fast, and May depicts sheep-tending, with rams, ewes and a sucking lamb. In June the mowing of grass takes place, in July wood is cut and loaded onto a cart with wattle sides, pulled by two oxen, and in August the reaping is done. The mowing, overseen by a figure with a horn, is done with sickles, and the same wattle-sided cart stands at hand. In September hogs are driven to mast by two figures with dogs, a horn and spears. Falconry is the occupation for October, a bonfire for November, and threshing and winnowing for December.

FARMING TOOLS

The tools shown in the pictures closely resemble hand tools still used on English farms. Very few identifiable examples have been discovered in archaeological sites. Whetstones have been found (as many as twelve at Uncleby, N Yorkshire) and small, sharpening steels with tangs for insertion into wooden handles. A 9in (23cm) pair of tongs or snippers was found at Sibertswold (Kent). Several sites have produced the metal edges, or 'shoes', with which wooden spades were shod. At Hurbuck (Co Durham) axes, a small pick and four scythe blades were found. The tangs of the scythes were originally bound to their shafts, exactly as in the manuscript pictures. *The Wise Reeve* also mentions many of the tools used in farming – axe, billhook, tughook, mattock, crowbar, ploughshare, coulter, harrowing-gear, goad, scythe, sickle, hoe, spade, shovel, woadspade, barrow, broom, hammer, rake, pitchfork, ladder, lantern, fire-tongs, weighing-machine, measure, flail, winnowing-fan, riddle, waggon-cover, seedbasket, horsecomb, shears, fodder-rack, and dung shovel. The list concludes: 'It is not within my power to describe everything a good reeve should attend to.'

PLOUGHING

Evidence of the ploughman's life comes from the *Colloquy* of Ælfric, eleventh-century abbot of Eynsham in Oxford. The *Colloquy* is really a conversational set-piece designed to exercise students of Latin by way of a discussion between a teacher and various imaginary workers – most of them manual labourers – as to which of their skills is the most necessary. The ploughman says:

I work very hard. At daybreak I drive the oxen out to the field and yoke them to the plough. No winter weather is so bitter that I dare lurk at home for fear of my lord, but when the oxen are yoked and the share and coulter fixed to the plough, I have to plough every day a full acre or more . . . I have a boy with me driving the oxen with a goad, who like me is now hoarse with the cold and the shouting . . . I have to fill the bins with hay for the oxen, water them and cart their dung away . . . It is very hard work because I am not a free man.

The calendar illustration shows the ploughman and his boy with a team of four oxen and a sower scattering his seeds broadcast. The care taken in showing the working parts of the plough suggests that the artist knew his subject well. A riddle in *The Exeter Book* of Anglo-Saxon poetry also refers to the plough.

My nose is downward: I go on my belly and dig into the ground, moving as directed by the grey enemy of the forest [the ox] and my master and protector, who walks stooping at my tail. He pushes me in the plain, lifts me and urges me on, and sows in my track. I nose my way forward, brought from the wood, put together with skill, carried on a waggon. I have many wonderful qualities. On one side of me as I travel there is green, and on the other my track is clear and black. Driven through my back and hanging down is a cunning spear. Another in my head, firm and projecting, falls to one side, so that I tear with my teeth if he who is my lord serves me well from behind.

LAND DIVISION

In a large part of England, the land which each man cultivated was not a compact holding, but scattered about in a number of places and worked according to the 'open-field' system. The system was devised because it was not possible to cultivate the fields year after year without exhausting the soil. The land was therefore divided into two or three roughly equal fields. Working in rotation, one of these was left fallow while the others were put to use. When the village fields were marked out, the whole area was divided into narrow strips of approximately one acre in area, a furlong ('furrow-long') in length, separated by grassy baulks. Where these were on hillsides, constant ploughing produced terraces of ridge and furrow which can still be seen. At the end of each group of strips, at right angles to the furrows, ran a 'headland' on which the plough was turned. The strips were allocated in such a way that everyone took a share of poorer land: Each man received a quantity of strips commensurate with the number of oxen he contributed to the plough team.

Individuals were not free to sow what they liked, for the rotation of crops was decided by the community. Under the three-field system, field 1 was sown in autumn with winter corn, wheat, or rye; field 2 early in the year with barley, beans, or oats, and field 3 lay fallow. Next year, field 1 would have the early sowing; field 2 would lie fallow, and field 3 would be sown in autumn, and so on in rotation. Under the two-field system, the one field in use each year was divided between autumn-sown and spring-sown crops. The fallow field was used for pasture, in the process of which it was manured, but the cultivated fields were fenced off until after harvest when the animals were allowed to graze on the stubble. Also fenced was the meadow – valuable hay-producing land usually beside a stream or river, which was shared like the arable land.

Woodland was valuable for fuel, timber and the pasturing of pigs. There was also common pasture and the common waste, sometimes used for grazing. Local practice varied considerably and the open-field system was not universal. In Kent and East Anglia, for example, farm holdings were more compact and rectangular in shape.

MILLING

In early days, milling was done by hand and a number of the querns used for this purpose can still be seen. Names such as Wharncliffe and Whernside (S and N Yorkshire) indicate places where hand quernstones were obtained. Animal-powered and water-driven mills later came into use, the former using 'mill-oxen', mentioned in a tenth-century charter associated with Thorney Abbey (Cambridgeshire). One of this type has been tentatively located at Cheddar, and a watermill at Old Windsor. The Domesday Book mentions over 5,000 watermills throughout England, and shows that some villages owned several, whilst others shared ownership with neighbouring villages. Names like Melbourne (Derbyshire) 'millstream' and many names beginning 'Mil-' or 'Mill-' go back to Anglo-Saxon times. Windmills did not come into use until after 1100.

Plate 1 Conventionalised labours of the months from an Anglo-Saxon calendar (BM MS Cotton Tiberius B V) eleventh century. The January picture gives us our most detailed illustration of an Anglo-Saxon plough. It is a two-handled wheel-plough, very short (perhaps because of limitations of space in the manuscript), with a shifting coulter and 'ear' to make all the furrows lie in one direction. The boy with the goad is urging the oxen on, and the sower is scattering seed.
The middle picture, for August, shows reaping with scythes and pitchforks almost identical with tools still in use. In the last picture, December, the corn is threshed by men with flails. One is winnowing – separating the chaff from the grain – and the figure on the right, perhaps the granary keeper, is recording the tally of baskets on a notched stick (British Library).

NCIPIT IAN... SANCTI TROPE CAPRICORNES

UARIUS HABET   DIES · XXX · I · LUNA · ...

A A KA A   P IANI URE KALENDARUM ĝes comcibitur agnus.

B B IIII N   Isidorus nonis gaudet mordine quadris.

B C C III N F   Sĉa genoueta trinis insanguine fulget.

D D ... ...

GUSTU MENSEM   LEO FERUIDUS IGNE PURIT

USTUS HABET   DIES · XXX · LUNA · XXIX ·

I Q C   AUG Macchabeus merito trabitur sepe kalende.

I C M R D III   R omsmquadris Stephanus preciderat alta.

S F III N   Y rinus iam Stephani pariuto inuencio sĉd.

T... ...IT ARC... urinis   medio sua fert a decembri

CEBER HABET   DIES · XXXI · LUNA · XXX ·

XIII OD ... ...   PRIMA DIES MENSIS KASIMUM CONTINET ALACUM.

II   A G IIII N   R tq; secunda dies auctorem possidet aequum

DOMESTIC ANIMALS

Two companions of the ploughman in the *Colloquy* are the oxherd and the shepherd. The oxherd describes how he leads the unyoked oxen to pasture, waters them and stands guard over them throughout the night for fear of thieves. His care indicates the value of these cattle to the farming community. Numerous laws were made to discourage their theft and misuse. A man had to make a public declaration of his ownership of livestock and call witnesses to vouch for him. If cattle were stolen, every man owning a horse was to ride in pursuit, and any suspect was to swear his innocence upon oath. In the time of Athelstan, the value of an ox was fixed at thirty silver pence and a cow at twenty. If a straying beast caused damage, the cost had to be borne by the man who had neglected his fences, while a dangerous and troublesome animal could be killed or become forfeit to the injured party.

Plate 2 Front panel of a Northumbrian carved whalebone box of about AD 700, known as the Franks Casket (after a former owner). The left-hand scene is from the legend of Wayland the smith. Wayland was hamstrung and forced to work for King Nithhad, but revenged himself by killing the king's sons and making goblets out of their skulls and jewels out of their eyes and teeth. The body of one of the princes is on the ground, his head in Wayland's tongs. The central figures are Nithhad's daughter and her maid. Wayland overcame the princess with drink, raped her, and then escaped on wings made from the feathers of birds – the incident depicted on the right.

The other scene shows the visit of the wise men to Jesus. The isolated word in the runes says 'magi'. The marginal runic inscription refers to the death of the whale which provided the bone: 'The sea lifted up the fish onto the shore; the whale became sad where he swam on the shingle. Whale's bone.' (Total length of panel 9in) (British Museum).

The shepherd of the *Colloquy* drives his flock to pasture in the early morning and, for fear of wolves, stands guard over it in heat and cold before leading it back to the fold. He milks his ewes twice a day, and makes cheese and butter. Several varieties of sheep are depicted in manuscripts, most of them horned, with long legs and long tails. They were valued at four pence and were of use not only for wool and meat but also for their skins, which could be used to make parchment.

Horses were more valuable than oxen, Athelstan's law setting the price of a good one at half a pound of silver. Fines for stealing horses were particularly heavy, and their export was legislated against by Athelstan. It is unlikely that the horse was used much as a draught animal, although one is shown pulling a harrow in the Bayeux Tapestry. They were certainly used in hunting and on military campaigns, although probably only for transport, not for cavalry action.

The other domestic animal of importance was the pig, valued at ten pence. In a will of about 880, two thousand of these animals were bequeathed by a nobleman called Alfred. Pigs in such numbers would require considerable pasturage. A man pasturing his pigs on another's land paid pannage (pasture fees) according to the quality of the mast wood. This amounted to every third pig if the pasture was so good that the bacon reached three fingers' thickness; every fourth if it was only two fingers thick. The owners of pigs which strayed paid fines of one shilling for each offence.

MEAT PRODUCTION

Some statistical analyses have been made of animal bones from Anglo-Saxon settlements, although a large-scale, systematic examination of representative sites has not yet been undertaken. The settlement at Maxey produced (by number): 36.5 per cent cattle bones; 36 per cent sheep or goat; 11 per cent pig; 8 per cent horse, and 8.5 per cent bird, as well as the bones of a dog and a cat. A rough estimate of the poundage of meat represented by these bones is: cattle 58 per cent; sheep or goat 11 per cent; pig only 5 per cent, and horse as much as 21 per cent. It seems that here the horse was slaughtered for meat before it reached old age, although the consumption of horsemeat was forbidden in 787 probably because of its association with heathen practices. 35 per cent of the cattle and 39 per cent of the sheep lived through at least two winters. Traditionally the Anglo-Saxons, like other early farming communities, are supposed to have killed off most of their stock before winter. However, the Maxey figures give no indication of slaughter on such a large scale.

At York, which in Anglo-Danish times rose on its refuse deposits above the floodwaters of the river Ouse, large numbers of bones have been excavated, and an analysis made of a small sample from Ousegate. Here, about 65 per cent (by weight) were chiefly leg and rib bones of cattle; 24 per cent red deer; the remainder including sheep, goats, pigs and hens. Other sites in the city have yielded the bones of horses, dogs, geese and ducks. The large numbers of red deer bones may be accounted for by the value of their horns, in the working of which there was a local industry. The considerable differences between Maxey, York and other places, such as Chalton, where cattle bones were infrequent, indicate the dangers of generalising about the practices of communities of differing dates and widely varying economies.

HUNTING, TRAPPING AND FISHING

Others lived off animals by hunting, trapping and fishing. In the *Colloquy* the king's hunter describes how he weaves and sets his nets, and trains his dogs to pursue wild beasts until they run into them. He also hunts harts, boars, fallow-deer and hares with his mixed pack of dogs and hounds. A boar is first flushed out by the hounds and eventually killed with a spear. All the game goes to the king, who in return clothes and feeds his man and sometimes gives him a horse or ring. The huntsman of Prince Æthelstan was rewarded at his master's death with a whole stud. Surviving wills also record bequests of hawks, and the moralising poem, *The Fates of Men*, describes how 'a man shall tame the proud wild bird, the hawk on the hand, until the falcon becomes gentle: he puts foot-rings on it and feeds it thus in fetters, proud in its plumage, weakens the swift flyer with little food until the wild bird becomes obedient to its master . . .' The *Colloquy* fowler also tames hawks. In autumn he selects suitable young birds which by winter he has fully trained. He prefers to set his hawks free in the spring when their demands for food become too great. During the summer this fowler depends on nets, nooses, birdlime, traps and decoy whistles.

His companion, the fisherman, works from a boat on the river with creels, nets and baited hooks. In this way he catches eels, pike, minnows, burbot, trout, lamprey and other fish for sale at market. At sea he catches, or collects, herring, salmon, porpoises, sturgeon, oysters, crabs, mussels, winkles, cockles, plaice, flounder and lobsters, but does not venture far out too often because he would need a large ship. He is aware that whaling is profitable, but fears the expense and the danger. Fish must have been consumed in large quantities, particularly on occasions when meat was prohibited by the church, and this fisherman remarks that he cannot catch as much as he could sell. The economic importance of this occupation is shown by the fact that payments were sometimes made in fish. A rental of land at Tidenham (Gloucestershire) included six porpoises and thirty thousand herrings annually, and King Edgar made a yearly gift to the monks at Ely of ten thousand eels. The Domesday Book shows that fisheries were sited at mill ponds throughout England but were especially concentrated in the Fenlands. An eleventh-century survey of the Tidenham estate mentions 101 basket-weirs and 4 hackle-weirs. At every weir each alternate fish belonged to the lord of the manor along with any rare fish which was of value. The weirs were built and maintained by tenants who had to supply forty large rods or a fother (cartload) of smaller ones for the purpose.

The archaeological evidence for all this hunting and fishing activity is confined to a small number of fish-hooks discovered at Sandtun (Kent), and fishbones which have been recognised at Chalton. Some placenames refer to the craft, for example Huntingdon, Fisherwick (Staffordshire) and Fullerton (Hampshire), 'fowlers' farm'.

MANUFACTURING

Manufacturing crafts were many and varied. There is evidence of soapmaking in the name Sapperton (Gloucestershire) and of charcoal production in names like Colwich (Staffordshire). Bellfounding has been traced in excavations at Winchester, plumbing at Mucking and Thetford, and bone- and horn-working at West Stow, where large numbers of combs and triangular rough-outs cut from red-deer antlers point to a cottage industry carried on between the fifth and seventh centuries. Common products of a similar industry in Anglo-Danish York were bone ice-skates made from the tibia of red deer, cattle and horses. They were fastened to the instep and ankle by means of thongs, and the

Fig 12   Bone skates from York – length 10in and 6½in

skater pushed himself along with an iron-shod pole. York also supported a thriving leather industry with tan-pits in Ousegate and Coppergate, and workshops producing shoes, laces, belts, garments, bags, knife-sheaths and gloves. The range of products referred to by the leatherworker of Ælfric's *Colloquy* is 'slippers and shoes, gaiters and leather bottles, reins and trappings, flasks and containers, spur-straps and halters, bags and purses'. In post-conversion times there were centres of stone sculpture at places like Hexham (Northumberland) and Bakewell (Derbyshire), although most work must have been done *in situ*. Bookmaking was a highly specialised monastic art involving the preparation of parchment, writing materials, pigments, bindings, book-clasps and, sometimes, jewelled covers.

Especially influential and productive were the scriptoria at Winchester and Canterbury.

It would take too long to describe all the techniques and crafts which were known and practised, but pottery, metalworking and woodworking were especially important and deserve particular attention.

POTTERY

There were probably few specialist potters in early Anglo-Saxon England. From the large numbers of unthrown, unglazed pots which survive, it seems likely that most households were capable of supplying their own needs. This was particularly true of the crude, undecorated domestic vessels. The best work was generally reserved for funeral urns which were often decorated with incised lines, bosses and stamps, and through a study of these it is possible to see that in the sixth century a trade in pots began to develop. Similar

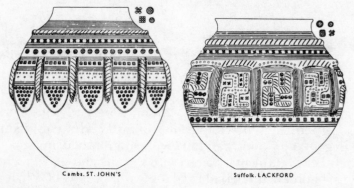

Cambs. ST. JOHN'S   Suffolk. LACKFORD

Fig 13   Burial urns with identical stamps, products of one workshop – height 13in and 12in (Clarendon Press – J. N. L. Myres, *Anglo-Saxon Pottery and the Settlement of England*)

examples of one potter's work, using identical stamps, have been found over eighty miles apart, at Lackford (Suffolk) and Thurmaston (Leicestershire), and, by the late sixth century, a workshop (probably near Lackford) was producing pots of standard size, shape and style, over a hundred specimens of which are known from various sites in East Anglia. A cruciform potter's stamp of this date, made from the tine of a red-deer antler was found at West Stow. Kilns of the pagan period have been discovered at Cassington (Oxfordshire). They consisted of a stoke-pit and firing-chamber, together about 10ft (3m) long, dug into gravel, with a kiln vault probably made by smearing clay and lime on a basket-frame of wattles.

The potter of later times was a much more competent craftsman whose operations centred upon such places as Ipswich, Thetford, Stamford (Lincolnshire) and Torksey – once an important commercial centre on the Trent in Lincolnshire, but now a quiet village. He had learned to work both a slow and fast wheel; his firing methods were more sophisticated and produced much harder, tougher pots; his repertoire of shapes and patterns had greatly increased and included vessels with spouts and handles, bottles, cresset-lamps, storage jars up to 3ft (0.9m) high, as well as the more common types. Most important of all, by the end of the period he had learned to glaze his pots, a development in which the Stamford workshop, with its light yellow, green and orange glazes, led the way.

METALWORKING

Iron ore was obtained from mines at Chester, Gloucester, Hereford, Northampton, and the counties of Somerset, Sussex and Yorkshire; lead from the mines of Derbyshire – all of which are mentioned in the Domesday Book. Place-names also refer to metal-extraction at Kirkby Overblow (N Yorkshire), in part from Old English *orblawere*, 'smelter'; Orrell (Manchester) meaning 'ore hill', Orgreave (S Yorkshire) and Orsett (Essex) recording 'ore-pits, pits where bog-ore is dug'. Examples of pits worked between 850 and 1150 have been identified at West Runton (Norfolk) where the ironstone pebbles were smelted in furnaces on the site. It has been calculated that the yield was small. Precious metals were often obtained by melting-down, or re-using, parts of ancient artefacts. For instance, the silver plates on the flanks of the Benty Grange Boar (Plate 8) were found to have been cut from a piece of antique silver – they were engraved on the reverse side with a Roman leaf-design. Imported metals sometimes came in the form of part-made goods, like quality swordblades from the Rhineland, to which decorated hilts of local manufacture were added. Blades inscribed with their makers' names 'Ulfberht' and 'Ingelrii' are found scattered throughout western Europe, including England.

The blacksmith is referred to in the names Smeaton (N Yorkshire) and Smisby (Derbyshire), and his smithy in Smeeth (Kent). Traces of his craft have been noted in a number of archaeological sites, among them Thetford and Winchester. In the *Colloquy* the disparaging question is asked of the smith: 'what do you give us in your smithy except fiery sparks of iron, din of banging sledgehammers and blowing bellows?' However, there can be no doubt of the smith's importance, for a law of King Ine permits a nobleman moving residence to take his smith with him, along with his reeve and children's nurse. A good smith would have been constantly in demand to make and repair implements, tools and domestic utensils. Besides this, he probably made the iron spearheads, scramasaxes and the bosses of the shields with which ordinary men went armed to battle. However, more elaborate arms – chainmail, jewelled swordhilts, inlaid blades, helmets – were the province of a specialist weaponsmith. One such specialist is referred to as a sword-furbisher *(sweordhwita)* in a law of Alfred, in which he is charged to return refurbished weapons in good condition. It has been suggested that the impressive whetstone/sceptre at Sutton Hoo alludes to the king in his role of provider and refurbisher of weapons.

But the finest work of all was undertaken by the goldsmith, whose skills can best be appreciated from surviving ornamental metalwork. That he was expert in the art of casting metal is evident from the many fine cast, and often gilded, brooches. He knew the art of beating and seaming bronze and silver sheets and castings into bowls and chalices, like the chalice from Trewhiddle (Cornwall), now in the

British Museum. He knew the techniques of engraving gold and silver, and of filling the grooves with *niello*, a black substance made from a mixture of metallic sulphides, to enhance the elaborate designs, as on the great gold buckle from Sutton Hoo. He understood the beauty of inlaying, in which gold, silver, or bronze was hammered into minute undercut furrows in a surface of iron or steel. The ninth-century Strickland Brooch in the British Museum is in gold-inlaid silver. He knew stamping, evident from the moneyer's craft, and the *repousse* process, seen on the Ormside Bowl in the Yorkshire Museum. In filigree work, the craftsman either twisted and plaited delicate threads of gold and silver wire into intricate patterns, or soldered minute granules of gold and silver on to a backplate, as on the tiny, pendant, gold cross from Winster (Derbyshire) now in Sheffield City Museum. Perhaps most remarkable are the *cloisonne* jewels. These were of two basic types, utilising either enamels or gemstones set into cells formed by small walls of gold or silver soldered to a backplate. A fine example of enamel *cloisonne* is the Alfred Jewel. Some of the best examples of gemstone *cloisonne* are shown in Plates 3 and 5. The goldsmith, of course, worked without aids such as magnifying glasses, and some of the best pieces may have taken years to make. It has been estimated that to cut or 'slice' the 450 garnets used in making a brooch from Abingdon may have taken one man about four or five months. Small wonder that the Anglo-Saxon craftsman's skill was recognised and sought after at home and abroad.

WOODWORKING

Less can be said about woodworking, for few wooden objects have survived. However, it is certain that in a society so dependent on timber the wright's skills were employed in tasks large and small, from the construction of boats and houses to the manufacture of furniture, tools and utensils. It is probably no accident that the Old English word for 'build' is *timbrian*. Wood shavings, wooden spoons and wooden combs are among the positive evidence for workshops in

York. Several bowls from there had been turned on a lathe. Surviving woodworking tools include axes, adzes, an auger, sawblades, a drawknife, a chisel and a carpenter's plane. The plane was found at Sarre (Kent) and is similar to a modern block-plane. It is 6in (15cm) long with a bronze bottom-plate, and has a hollow in the antler stock for the user's fingers.

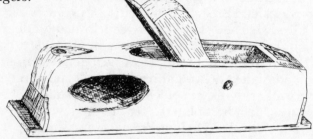

Fig 14   Reconstruction of plane from Sarre, Kent – length 6in

The shipwright's skill is best demonstrated by the Sutton Hoo ship, or rather by the impression the vessel left in the sand of the burial mound, for the timbers themselves had decayed. It was about 89ft (27m) long, clinker-built with nine strakes a side and, apparently, no permanent decking. The strakes were 1in (2.5cm) thick, each made of several lengths of timber riveted together at overlapping joints, or scarfs, and fixed to the ribs by means of pegs and bolts. The ship was steered by a large paddle or side-rudder at the stern and powered by forty oarsmen. There was no indication of a mast or permanent sail. Only three other Anglo-Saxon boats are known – another from Sutton Hoo, one from Snape

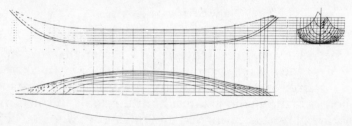

Fig 15   The lines of the Sutton Hoo ship – length about 89ft *(The Sutton Hoo Ship Burial: A Handbook)*

(Suffolk) and one recently discovered at Graveney (Kent). The Bayeux Tapestry depicts several stages of boatbuilding, from the felling of trees to the fitting-out, the workmen employing axe, adze, hammer and drill.

WOMEN'S WORK

Although a woman might occupy a position of power or influence, be active in diplomacy, or own and run extensive estates, the day-to-day matters of domestic economy were also her domain. If she was of low status she would be directly involved in activities like cooking and baking, lending a hand with the threshing, and tending the household fire, just as depicted in the Riddles. Women's graves, besides furnishing a variety of domestic vessels and utensils, have produced iron 'strike-a-lights' which were struck against flint to produce a spark. A rich woman would have servants to perform such menial household tasks for her, not necessarily women – the cook and the baker of Ælfric's *Colloquy* are men. The domestic utensils with which a woman might concern herself on a large estate are listed in *The Wise Reeve*. They include pots, pans, cauldron, kettle, ladle, jars, flagons, dishes, jugs, tub, bath, cask, keg, churn, cheesevat, honeybin, beerbarrel, strainer, candlestick, saltcellar, pepperhorn, stools, lantern, soapbox, firescreen, and firedogs. In particular, a woman kept the household keys and sometimes carried them with her to the grave. Surviving ones are between 2½ and 6½in (6-16cm) long, usually of iron. At one end they have a projection at right angles to the stem, and at the other a ring for suspension. Items such as keys may have been attached to bronze 'girdle-hangers' which are a feature of female burials especially in Anglian areas, but because of their apparent impracticality it has been suggested that girdle-hangers were no more than symbols of domestic authority. Padlocked boxes have been found in rich women's graves such as that at Cowlow (Derbyshire). A law of Cnut explicitly states a woman's responsibility for the household goods. If a man was found to have stolen property in his home his wife was not considered a party to

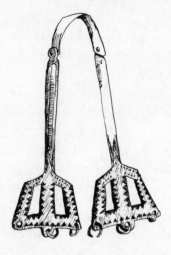

Fig 16   Bronze 'girdle-hanger'

the crime 'unless it be brought under the woman's lock and key. . . . It is her duty to keep the keys of her storeroom, her chest and her cupboard. If it is brought into any of these, then she is guilty'.

Clothmaking and embroidery were common occupations for women of all ranks. This is made clear in one of the penitentials of Theodore, Archbishop of Canterbury, in which women are specifically forbidden to work on Sundays either in weaving, cleaning or sewing vestments, carding wool, beating flax, washing garments, shearing sheep, or in any such occupations.

SPINNING AND WEAVING

Spinning particularly was so much a part of women's work that it gave rise to an alliterative phrase, 'the spear-side and the spindle-side'. King Alfred in his will said that his grandfather had bequeathed his lands *on þa spere healfe* and not *on þa spinl healfe*, and that he himself proposed to do the same and pass his land to his male descendants. Bone pins up to about 6in (15cm) long, like those from Barrington (Cambridgeshire), have been tentatively identified as spindles. More common are the small pierced discs of bone or stone used to steady the spindle, known as spindle-whorls. These are found in cemeteries and dwellingplaces in all areas and from all periods.

Weaving was done mainly on an upright loom, the two main supports of which were sometimes set deep into the ground. Post-holes from such looms, together with numerous annular, clay loom weights, with which the warp threads were weighted, have enabled weaving huts to be identified at many archaeological sites, among them Old Erringham, Sutton Courtenay and West Stow. The weights are sometimes deposited in rows, as if the loom had for some reason been threaded when abandoned. An object sometimes found in rich women's graves is the iron weaving sword, used in 'beating-up' the surface of woven material. Nine examples are known from cemeteries in the south and east of England. The one from Finglesham (Kent) was 20¾in (52.5cm) long and 'pattern-welded' (p 124) as if it had been made from an old military sword. A late example from Wallingford Castle is made of bone and carries an inscription in Old English. From documents, the list of clothmaking implements may be expanded. *The Wise Reeve*, for example, mentions flax-lines, spindles, reels, bobbins, presses, shuttles, needles and sleek-stones. The noise and activity of the weaving room is evoked in a riddle in which a coat-of-mail speaks of the paradox that its 'weave' is not produced on a loom: 'Wefts are not wound in me, nor do I have any warp, nor does the thread resound in me through the force of many strokes, nor does the whirring shuttle glide in me, nor the weaver's rod strike me anywhere'.

EMBROIDERY

'A woman's place is at her embroidery' says one of the poetic *Maxims*, and certainly there is good evidence for her activity and achievement in this field. Graves have produced small needlecases or workboxes – cylindrical containers about 2½in (6cm) high with a hinged lid and sometimes a chain for suspension. They are made of bronze, often with simple geometrical ornament, and sometimes gilded. One

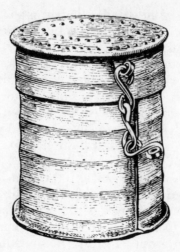

Fig 17 Bronze workbox from Kirby Underdale – height 2½in
(British Museum – *Guide to Anglo-Saxon Antiquities in the BM*)

from Kingston contained two gilt-bronze needles; one from
Uncleby two kinds of thread, and one from Kempston (Bedfordshire) fragments of cloth. The small shears, tweezers,
prickers and knives often found in graves may be connected
with embroidery.

Outstanding finished products are the stole, maniple and
girdle from the Tomb of St Cuthbert, and the Bayeux
Tapestry itself. The St Cuthbert vestments, which were made
in Wessex at the beginning of the tenth century, show
prophets and other subjects delicately embroidered in
coloured silks and couched gold thread upon a foundation
fabric of silk. The Bayeux Tapestry was probably, though
not certainly, designed and worked in England. Technically
an embroidery since the figures are sewn on to the fabric
rather than woven into it, it is less sumptuous than the
vestments, but a remarkable achievement nonetheless on
account of its size and the spirit and deftness with which it
treats an important historical subject. It is 77yd long and
20in wide (70m by 50cm), embroidered in coloured wools on
plain linen in laid and couched work supplemented with
stem- and outline-stitching.

Items like this, as well as the gold braids of earlier times, were often produced by women of rank and leisure, but sewing was by no means confined to this class, for in the will of Wynflæd two slaves are bequeathed, one a weaver and one a seamstress. By the time of the Norman Conquest the beautiful garments of the English nobility had come to be so much admired that the anonymous author of a life of William the Conqueror asserted that English women excelled all others in needlework and in the art of embroidery with gold. Another contemporary writer, William of Poitiers, explains that fine embroidery was so characteristic that it was distinguished by the name *Anglicum opus*, 'English work'.

4

How They Organised Their Society

Two of the cardinal principles of the Anglo-Saxon social hierarchy were the bonds of loyalty between a man and his lord and between a man and his family. However, loyalty to one's lord came first.

This was no abstract principle, but a practical obligation of mutual protection which had been fundamental to order and justice for centuries. Tacitus wrote of the Germans that

> On the field of battle it is a disgrace for the chief to be surpassed in bravery by his retainers, and for the retainers not to equal the bravery of their chief. To have left the battle alive after the chief has been killed means lifelong infamy and shame. To defend and protect him, and to assign their own acts of strength to his credit, is to them true loyalty. The chief fights for victory, the retainers for their chief.

Nine hundred years later the same sentiments are expressed in *The Battle of Maldon*, a poem which celebrates the heroic stand of Byrhtnoth and the men of Essex against a Viking army in 991. After heavy fighting Byrhtnoth falls dead in the thick of the action, thanking God for the glory of that day. His loyal retainers wish only to lose their lives alongside him or to avenge their dead lord. 'My loss is the greatest,' shouts Ælfwine, 'for he was both my kinsman and my lord', and Leofsunu adds: 'The brave warriors around

Plate 3 *(overleaf)* Jewelled gold brooch from Kingston, Kent. It is made of two round gold plates, 3¼in in diameter fixed ¼in apart. The space between is filled with white paste. The decoration of the front is mainly of garnets set in *cloisons* (cells), their lustre enhanced by a backing of hatched gold foil (visible where the stones have been lost). Some *cloisons* are filled with lapis lazuli and there are panels of granule filigree. The regularly spaced round bosses are made of a white shell-like material topped with garnets. At the back are a safety-loop and a bronze pin, jewelled with garnets. The brooch, dating from the seventh century, was found in the grave of a rich woman buried in a coffin within a barrow. There were also two silver brooches, a gold pendant, a pottery beaker, a glass cup and two bronze bowls. Bones of a child from an earlier burial had been gathered together at her feet (Merseyside County Museums, Liverpool).

Plate 4 *(overleaf)* Jewelled gold brooch from Winster Moor, Derbyshire. A provincial craftsman's attempt at manufacturing, at a slightly earlier date, the type of brooch shown above. The petal-shaped garnets fit less neatly into their gold cells, and the gold filigree is cruder. Behind the 2in gold disc at the front is another, the same size but of silver, fixed closely to it by rivets under the four circular *cabochon* garnets near the edge. There is no means of attachment. The brooch was found by a farmer about 1765 in a barrow called White Low, along with two glass vessels, a silver bracelet, several beads and the metal fittings of a wooden box in which the objects had been buried (Sheffield City Museum).

Plate 5 *(left)* Jewelled gold shoulder-clasps from the Sutton Hoo ship burial. Each pair is 4½in long and hinges on a gold pin. They were sewn to a cloth or leather garment by means of the strong gold staples at the back, and were probably part of the regalia of a king. Decoration is in *cloisonné* garnets and coloured *millefiori* glass. Many design features are distinctive of the Sutton Hoo master-craftsmen. Some of the garnets appear to be set into solid gold, an effect achieved by capping the background *cloisons* with gold lids. The use of naturalistic subjects, like the interlaced serpents and the interlinked boars at the ends, is unparalleled on garnet jewellery found outside Sutton Hoo, and nowhere else are such large plate-garnets used. The serpents and the mosaic of 'carpet-pattern' foreshadow the decoration of the earliest illuminated manuscripts later in the seventh century (British Museum).

Sturmere will have no need to reproach me, now that my friendly lord lies dead, that I journeyed home lordless or broke away from the battle; but weapons shall take my life, spear-point and sword-blade'. Then another man, Byrhtwold, makes a declaration just before he is killed, which is taken as the classic expression of heroic defiance:

> *Our spirits shall be sterner, hearts the keener, courage*
> *the greater as our strength fades. Here on the ground lies*
> *our lord, a good man cut down. The man who thinks of*
> *leaving the battle now shall regret it for ever. I am old. I*
> *will not run away, but intend to lie dead alongside my*
> *lord, by so dear a man.*

The Battle of Maldon is an idealised description by one who presumably was not present at the fight, but it would be wrong to dismiss its sentiments as unrealistic. The *Anglo-Saxon Chronicle* and other histories record many vendettas in which the injured party doggedly stuck to its principles, as when in 786 the retainers of Cynewulf fought to the death to avenge their dead lord, scornfully refusing all offers to negotiate. There are also stories of treachery which show that the ideals were not always upheld. Even at Maldon, the sons of Odda took flight, Godric riding off on his fallen lord's horse 'though it was not right', and in 757 the king of Mercia was murdered by his own bodyguard. There are accounts, too, of men without lord or family who could offer no loyalty and expect no protection in return. A poem called *The Wanderer* tells of the plight of a man whose lord has died, and the poetic *Maxims* tell us: 'Wretched is the man who must live alone. Fate has decreed that he shall live without relatives. It would be better for him if he had a brother'.

Eventually a system was evolved to mitigate the wasteful effects of feuding by allowing the payment of *wergild* – literally 'man-price' – the compensation to be paid in atonement for a man's killing. Money settlement could be made without loss of honour provided the proper conditions of payment were met. It was officially encouraged as being a more equitable, charitable and controllable form of justice than the blood feud. The classes of *wergild* varied with time and place, but the most usual in Wessex were the 'twelve hundred (shillings) men', the 'six hundred men', and the 'two hundred men'. An elaborate scheme of compensation for injury was also devised. Alfred's laws stipulate payments of thirty shillings for an ear struck off (double if deafness resulted), sixty for a nose, four for a back tooth knocked out, eight for a front tooth, thirty for a thumb cut off, nine for a little finger (one for the nail alone) and twenty for a big toe.

CLASSES OF SOCIETY

A man's *wergild* established his legal status but was only an approximate indication of his standing in society. There were further class divisions based upon birth, wealth, rights, duties and occupation. The most commonly distinguished classes are king, nobleman (thane, *ealdorman* or *gesith*), free peasant (churl) and slave.

Legally the king was supreme within his kingdom, but he might be subject to a more powerful neighbour king. Athelstan, who ruled from 924 to 939, has the best claim to be called the first king of all England. The early war leaders probably ruled by strength, and even in later times we learn of weak kings being driven out, like Æthelred 'the Unready' in 1013. *Unræd* really means 'without counsel' or 'ill-advised'. The king was elected (usually from among the royal family) by a council of great lords. His right was all the stronger if he could claim to trace his ancestry back to the founder of the kingdom and, in pagan times, to the gods. Lineage was often emphasised by the choice of a name which alliterated with those of predecessors, such as Cerdic, Cynric, Ceawlin, and so on. In Christian times the church upheld the dignity and sanctity of the king, and in the eighth century the custom of ecclesiastical coronation was introduced.

In early times, a king's man transferred to his lord not only his acquisitions, but also the credit and honour of his exploits. Beowulf, for instance, presents to Hygelac the armour which he has been given for destroying the troll, Grendel. A type of death-duty paid in later times developed out of the practice of returning *heriot*, loaned war-gear, to the king or lord at a man's death. For example, the will of Bishop Theodred in the tenth century begins 'First, he grants his [royal] lord his heriot, that is, two hundred marks of red gold, and two silver cups, and four horses, the best I have, and the two best swords I have, and four shields, and four spears, and the land I have at Duxford, Illington and Arrington'. For his part the king gave generous gifts of gold and rings to his men, earning himself epithets such as 'gold-friend' and 'treasure-giver', and also gifts of land. Like any other lord he also offered protection backed up with the force of law.

A nobleman was distinguished from a peasant freeman, firstly by the property he owned, and secondly by birth. One document speaks of a time when 'if a peasant prospered so that he had fully five hides of land of his own, a church and a kitchen, a bellhouse and a castlegate, a seat and a special office in the king's hall, then he was henceforth worthy of the status of a nobleman'. A 'hide' was a measure of land (its size varying from kingdom to kingdom) supposed to be sufficient to provide the needs of one family. This land requirement seems to have been all-important. Another document says that even if a peasant did so well as to possess helmet, mailcoat and gold-adorned sword 'if he does not have the land he is still a peasant'. If the land requirement was met over a number of years by a man, his son and his grandson, then noble status became hereditary. Noblemen sometimes possessed extensive and widely scattered estates and travelled from one to another living for a time on each, as did the king on his royal manors.

Despite the disproportionate attention given to the upper classes in literature and documents, there can be no doubt that the backbone of society was the free peasant or churl, the 'two hundred (shilling) men' of the West Saxon laws. The churl inherited and owned land, had status in law, and could go where he wished; in return he paid his dues to the crown and church and took part in the folkmoot and in military service. Anglo-Saxon laws depict him collaborating with his neighbours in sharing his ox-team and helping in the fencing of fields. However, we should not have too idealised a view of the Anglo-Saxon peasant. A man might prosper and better himself, as we have seen, but the situation of the free peasant tended to deteriorate as time passed. If the land he owned failed to provide sufficient for himself and his dependants, he might have to lease further land from a lord and pay for it in produce or in service.

Some of the rents and services by which land was held are listed in the document called *The Rights of Various People*. The *geneat* ('companion') paid rent and performed many of the duties of reeve or bailiff – riding and carrying, accompanying his lord, attending to hedges, fences and hides for hunting deer, caring for horses and conducting strangers to the village. The *cottar* paid no rent, but worked for his lord each Monday throughout the year and three days a week at harvest time, in return for the five acres or so which he held. The *gebur* paid his dues in money and produce and had numerous duties to perform. He worked on his lord's land weekly for two or three days and ploughed at least one acre a week for him, took his turn at the sheepfold and his share in maintaining hunting dogs. In his first year of service he was set up with two oxen, one cow, six sheep, seven acres of sown land, tools for his work and utensils for his house. At the man's death all he possessed was taken back by his lord, who also maintained workmen like the herdsmen, beekeeper, cheesemaker, granaryman, woodward and hedgekeeper. Besides their duties, these men had special perquisites – shoes and gloves for the oxherd, every tree blown down by the wind for the woodward, and so on.

At the lowest social level was the unfree man, the slave. He had no *wergild*, only a price, equivalent in value to eight oxen. He was simply a chattel, and could be bought, sold and bequeathed – as in the will which grants two men along with ten oxen and instructs 'let them follow the lordship to which the land belongs'. A man could be born to serfdom or become enslaved through bad luck or misdemeanour. The Vikings and other enemies sometimes seized whole families to sell into slavery abroad, and in hard times a free household might itself sell some of its members to escape starvation. In one document, a lady records the release of 'all the men whose persons (literally "heads") she took so that they might obtain food in the evil days'. Enslavement was also a legal punishment. If, for instance, a freeman worked on Sunday, he had to pay a sixty-shilling fine according to a law of Ine, but if unable to pay was reduced to slavery. A slave had practically no rights and, unless his owner was prepared to pay fines and compensation on his behalf, was punished for crimes by capital or corporal means, such as scourging, castration, hanging, or stoning to death. One of Alfred's laws shows that they were permitted to own a little property. It grants 'the four Wednesdays in the four Ember weeks as holidays to all slaves to sell to whomever they wish that which any man has given them in God's name or which they are able to earn in any of their spare time'. They were sometimes able to buy their freedom or have it bought for them. Slaves also absconded, perhaps to join an adventuring Viking host, but the more common route to freedom in late Anglo-Saxon times was through manumission. In many wills there are instructions for their release: 'let all my men go free in my household and on my estate for my own soul and for those who begot me'. Freed slaves did not automatically acquire the rights of freemen by birth, but with the decline in peasant status on the one hand and manumission of serfs on the other, class divisions at the lower end of the social scale became increasingly less marked.

ADMINISTRATION

The consolidation of the English kingdoms was assisted by the evolution of a legislative and administrative system through which the powers of the king might be felt throughout the country. At its head was the king's council, his *witan*, 'wisemen', made up of lay and ecclesiastical magnates who advised on matters of policy, law, land grants and taxation. It met most often at great festival times, sometimes in towns but often in smaller places, such as whichever royal country residence the king happened to be in at the time. With the advice of the council the king issued laws, charters and writs by which the will of the government was made known.

The highest royal official was the *ealdorman* whose title was eventually superseded by *eorl* (earl). He was chosen for life, usually from one of the great families, and was normally responsible for one or several shires. He presided at the district assembly, imprisoned thieves, regulated feuds and led the local levies in time of war. Byrhtnoth, who commanded the English at Maldon, was *ealdorman* of Essex, and the army he led was formed partly of his own retainers, his *heorthgeneatas*, 'hearth-companions', but mostly of the conscripted local militia called the *fyrd*.

Below the *ealdormen* were the king's reeves, who, if in charge of a single shire, were called 'shire-reeves', later 'sheriffs'. The reeves' main duties were to run the king's estates, officiate at the *folc-gemot*, or people's meeting, regulate traders, supervise moneyers, exact fines and dues, witness property deals, trace stolen cattle, lead the attack on powerful wrongdoers, and fight along with the *fyrd*. There were also town-reeves who served the king. When the first Vikings landed, about 789, it was the reeve of Dorchester who rode out to ask them their business and was killed by them for thus doing his duty.

The king derived his income partly from the royal estates and partly from fines, forfeitures, inherited property and customary dues. In a similar way the *ealdorman* and reeve benefited from estates with which the king rewarded them for their duties, and took a share in other revenues. The upkeep of the king's court was made possible by his 'farm', a food-rent which developed from the practice by which subjects entertained their king as he moved about the country. This 'farm' was originally sufficient to maintain the king and his retinue for twenty-four hours and was usually paid in provisions such as ale, meat, cheese and grain. The king and his servants also had traditional rights to hospitality and other services from landowners, such as safe conduct of messengers and hospitality to huntsmen.

PUBLIC SERVICE

Exemption from these duties could sometimes be bought, but this was rarely the case with the three basic public services of military duty, fortification work and bridge repair. The laws of Athelstan required two well mounted men for each plough for military service, but, in 1006, so great was the threat to the kingdom that Æthelred 'had the whole of the people of Wessex and Mercia called out, and they were on service against the Vikings all the autumn, but with no more success than very often in the past'. Earlier, military success had been achieved by Alfred and his descendants through systematic building and manning of fortresses throughout the country. By the early tenth century, few villages south of the Thames were more than twenty miles from such a refuge, and the building programme was extended northwards in the wake of successful campaigns against the Danes. Each fortress, or *burh*, was repaired and garrisoned by men of the district, one man for every 4ft (1.3m) of wall or earthwork – a heavy commitment, but one which proved effective. The third duty of bridge building and repair was also apportioned amongst owners of land in the locality and was worked out in great detail. At Rochester, responsibility was separately allotted for the upkeep of the individual piers of the bridge, together with the adjacent supporting beams and a fixed length of planking.

Provision and maintenance of a naval force was a further duty to which the landowners had to contribute, especially in the reign of Æthelred. But the hardest burden at this time must have been the special tribute-payment called Danegeld, by which the Anglo-Saxons attempted to buy off the attacks of the Danes. Records of 10,000 silver pounds paid in 991; 24,000 in 1002, and 48,000 in 1011, as well as great quantities of Anglo-Saxon coins found in Denmark, many of which are now in the Royal Collection in Copenhagen, point as much to the fruitlessness of Danegeld as to its effect upon the country's economy.

MONEY AND TRADE

The main denominations of Anglo-Saxon coinage were the *sceat*, the *penig* (penny) and the *styca*. The gold *solidus*, a seventh-century imitation of a Roman coin, was perhaps the earliest coin to be struck, but it may have been used simply as ornament, not as currency. The earliest widely used coins were the *sceattas*, small and thick, sometimes of gold but more commonly of silver, which were probably introduced about 695. In the eighth century, the *sceat* was replaced by the larger, thinner penny, which became almost the sole denomination south of the Humber for the next five hundred years. The coin issued in Northumbria, until it also was replaced by the penny, was the *styca*, which was like the *sceat* in shape but made of base silver later degenerating to copper. Several denominations mentioned in documents, such as the pound, mark, *mancus* and shilling, were not current coins but simply money of account. The pound was worth 240 pennies or 250 *sceattas*, the mark (a Danish weight) half a pound, the *mancus* (a weight of gold) one eighth of a pound or 30 pence. The value of the shilling varied according to district – 48 to the pound in Wessex and 60 in Mercia. The following are some approximate comparative values in the reign of Athelstan: a slave, one pound; a horse, half a pound; an ox, one *mancus*; a cow, 20 pence; a pig, 10 pence; a shank of bacon, 4 pence; a sheep, one shilling (probably Mercian, therefore worth 4 pence).

The increasing complexity of trade, both at home and abroad, was the main reason for the development of the coinage, but even in earlier times trading was quite highly developed. Salt and metals were essential requirements for which traffic with some coastal and mining areas would have been necessary. Supplies of fish from the coastal districts probably began early. There is archaeological evidence that internal trade in pottery and jewellery had developed before the end of the pagan period, and that imports included gold, glass, garnets, wine and swordblades. The seventh-century Sutton Hoo ship-mound, in particular, contained many foreign items acquired by trade or gift. Less is known about exports, although slaves were certainly among the earliest. Pope Gregory advised, in the sixth century, that English boys be bought in Gaul to be trained to assist in the conversion of England, and the famous story of the Angles whom he encountered in a Roman market and likened to angels, shows that they might be traded far from their homeland. Foreign trade in slaves continued illegally to the end of the Anglo-Saxon period, and a sermon by Wulfstan, an eleventh-century archbishop of York, complains that kinsmen even sold abroad relatives whom they were morally obliged to support. By this time trading had become quite sophisticated and centred mostly upon the fortified boroughs. The imaginary merchant of Ælfric's *Colloquy* gives an impression of the rich merchandise which passed through them: 'purple garments and silk, precious jewels and gold, rare apparel and perfume, wine and oil, ivory and brass, copper and tin, sulphur and glass, and many such things'. A merchant was a man of status, and we are told that if he crossed the sea three times at his own expense he was entitled to the rank of nobleman.

LAW

Anglo-Saxon law differed from modern systems in that more importance was attached to the weight of a man's oath than to establishing the facts of the alleged crime. The value of a man's oath depended upon his rank and was closely related to his *wergild*. A highborn man could also expect more compensation for wrong or injury than could a man of lesser status, but fines and forfeitures for his own misdemeanours were likewise proportionately greater.

Legal procedure was strictly regulated and a man who failed to act according to the rules lost his case. What usually happened was that the plaintiff made his charge public with an oath to the effect that he was not motivated merely by malice. The nature of the accusation determined the weight of the oath needed to deny it. For instance, it is laid down in the laws issued jointly by Alfred and the Danish King Guthrum:

If anyone accuses a king's thane (noble servant) of homicide, if he dares to clear himself let him do it with the oaths of twelve king's thanes; if anyone accuses a man of lower rank than king's thane, let him clear himself with the oaths of eleven of his equals and one king's thane.

If the requisite number of compurgators could be produced to swear on a man's behalf he was judged to have proved his innocence and the case was ended. If the accused man failed to appear to answer the charges brought against him he lost his case, and if he or his relatives failed to pay the appropriate fines or compensation the man became an outlaw and could be hunted down and killed. In certain circumstances, such as when a man had been caught in the act or had committed his crime before witnesses, he was denied the right of oath. Instead, his accusers were required to swear to what they had seen.

As a last resort the accused might go to the ordeal, a physical trial administered by the church in which it was believed that God would protect the innocent. After a three-day fast, he was given a last chance to confess at a solemn mass and then proceeded to one of three tests – by cold water, hot water, or hot iron. In the first of these the accused was bound and lowered into consecrated water. If he sank more than one and a half ells (5½ft, 1.7m) he was cleared, but if he floated it was considered that the water had cast up the evil and his guilt was established. The ordeals of hot water and iron took place within the church itself. In the first the man had to plunge his hand into a cauldron of boiling water, either up to the wrist or to the elbow depending on the severity of the ordeal, take out a stone and carry it 9ft (2.7m); in the latter a red-hot iron weight of one or three pounds was carried. The hand was then wrapped and if found to be clean and not festering after three days the man's innocence was considered established.

Surviving laws make provision for a variety of crimes of which the following are some of the most common: absconding of slaves, accessory to an unlawful act, adultery, bribery, breach of the peace, breach of sanctuary, failure to observe holy days, harbouring criminals, heathen practices, homicide, neglect of military service, neglect leading to damage, malpractice of moneyers, perjury, sex crimes and, most common of all, theft. Punishments ranged from death to reparation. The nature of the death penalty depended on the circumstances of the crime.

Hanging was the usual method but we also hear of decapitation, drowning (of a witch and female slave) and being thrown from a cliff (for a female thief). In Athelstan's reign, a female slave found guilty of theft was burned on a fire prepared by eighty other slaves; a male slave convicted of the same offence was stoned to death by twenty-six others, any of whom was scourged if he failed three times to hit the man. Mutilation by striking off hand or foot was the punishment for a churl caught in the act of theft. A moneyer who issued false coins had his hand chopped off and fastened outside his mint as an example to others. Fines and forfeitures were a common punishment, the proceeds usually going to the king, his officials, or the church. Compensation was usually paid to the injured party, but sometimes others took a share, as when the king retained two-thirds of a slain foreigner's *wergild*. Reduction to slavery was prescribed for one who could not pay the fine or compensation demanded of him. For some offences a man might be imprisoned – for instance, forty days for minor perjury. The offender was kept in the custody of a king's reeve on one of the royal estates, and the cost of his food was borne by himself or his relatives.

THE FAMILY

Most of the laws relating to family matters were probably customary and were never written down. It is also likely that custom changed as ecclesiastical influence developed, for in such matters as the affinity of kindred we notice a gradual hardening of attitude. On this subject Germanic tradition was at odds with Christian law and, from a letter, reported by Bede, in which Augustine sought advice from Pope Gregory, we can see that it was one of the first problems of the early missionaries. Gregory advised that 'it must be the third or fourth generation of the faithful that can lawfully be joined in matrimony', but in later times marriage was forbidden within the sixth degree and participants in illicit unions were excommunicated. But the marriage procedure itself probably changed little over the years except that ecclesiastical solemnisation came to be encouraged.

It was in two parts – the pledge (Old English *wed*) and the gift. A man wishing to obtain the consent of the woman and her kinsmen first pledged his honourable intentions, naming a suitable remuneration to her guardian for which his friends stood surety. When the terms were agreed the gift of the bride took place. The day after consummation it was customary to present the bride with a 'morning gift' which remained strictly her own property and among the wealthy sometimes took the form of a gift of land to provide her with a cash income.

One of the earliest written Kentish laws seems to imply that a wife could be purchased almost as chattel:

> *If a freeman lies with another freeman's wife, let him pay for it with his* wergild *and get another wife at his own expense and bring her to the other man's home.*

But elsewhere her own willingness is made an essential requirement.

The same code of laws also makes very simple provision for divorce, stating that 'if she wishes to depart with her children she shall have half the family wealth'. If the husband wished to keep the children, the wife was still entitled to her half. Other laws were framed to protect a wife who was not accessory to her husband's misdeeds. She retained one-third of the property of a convicted thief and was not punished for handling meat stolen by her husband 'because she must obey her lord', provided that she was able to swear on oath that she herself had not eaten any. On the other hand, any exposed complicity of the family meant that the whole household could be committed to slavery. Children became of age at ten or twelve years and could then own property and be punished for their offences. According to a law of Athelstan, no one under fifteen was subject to capital punishment.

Land was normally inherited by a man's sons or, in the absence of these, by his daughters, unless it was 'bookland'. This is the name for land taken from common ownership and granted by written charter to a private owner. In this case it could be freely bequeathed along with other possessions. If a man died leaving a wife and child, the law held that the child should accompany the mother, and that one of the father's kinsmen should act as guardian to take care of his property until he reached the age of ten. Family ties were strong, and a watchful interest was taken in the affairs of close relatives. It was the family that settled terms of marriage, assisted its members in court, maintained them when in prison, followed up blood feuds, and exacted suitable compensation.

At the end of our period men sometimes formed themselves into socio-religious fraternities of mutual aid, called guilds, the surviving statutes of which deal with such matters as fetching home a sick man, providing a respectable funeral, recompense for injury, pursuit of feuds, contributions towards pilgrimage expenses, compensation for fire-loss and common almsgiving. The guilds presumably offered security and protection to those who were insufficiently provided for by more traditional means, such as lord and family. But the principles of help and self-help are precisely those which are at the foundation of the earliest Anglo-Saxon society.

5

What They Believed

IN the passage of his *Germania* which deals with the Angli, the continental ancestors of the Angles, Tacitus speaks of a goddess called Nerthus, a mother-earth deity, worshipped by them in the first century after Christ:

> *On an island in the ocean there is a sacred wood, and in it a consecrated chariot covered by a vestment. Only one priest is allowed to touch it. He knows when the goddess is present in her sanctuary and attends her with great reverence as she is drawn along by cows. Happy are the days and festive the places wherever she condescends to go and be received. They do not fight battles or carry arms; every weapon is put aside; peace and quiet are only then known and loved, until the same priest returns the goddess to her temple when she is weary of contact with mortals. Soon afterwards the chariot and the vestments and, if you are willing to believe it, the deity herself are washed in a secret lake. This rite is performed by slaves who are immediately drowned in the lake, from which a mysterious dread and pious ignorance develops as to what this thing can be which is seen only by those about to die.*

Worship of Nerthus, or similar deities, along the lines of the rites described here, is proved by the survival, in north European peat bogs, of corpses of men and women who seem to have suffered some sort of ritual murder. The best known example is the corpse of a man found at Tollund (Denmark) who had been strangled and hanged with a leather rope before being thrown into the bog. A man at Grauballe (Denmark) had had his throat cut. The last meal of both men had been entirely vegetable, of a type perhaps specially prepared for sacrificial victims. The Grauballe man had last eaten a gruel which contained the seeds of over sixty-three varieties of wild and cultivated plants. Finds and records of peat-bog corpses up to 1965 number: 166 from Denmark; 69 from Schleswig-Holstein (traditional home of the Angles); 146 from the area of north Germany from which the Saxons probably migrated, and a further 48 from Holland. Not all of these were sacrificial victims, but there are sufficient to show that, on the eve of their migration to Britain, some of the Anglo-Saxons' ancestors practised fertility rites involving human sacrifice along with sacrifice of waggons, weapons, vessels and other objects also found in the bogs.

PAGAN MYTHOLOGY

Little evidence has survived from pre-Christian England of a systematic mythology, that is, of any organised attempt to express a view of the universe in stories about gods and devils. It is true that some of the old gods' names are known, and that these are related to the names of gods in Scandinavian mythology whose exploits are mainly recorded in the *Eddas* and sagas of Iceland, but it is wrong to assume too easily that, because the Anglo-Saxons and Scandinavians are racially related, the beliefs of fifth- and sixth-century England were necessarily close to those of Scandinavia which were only written down about 600 years later.

It seems from the names of the weekdays that the Anglo-Saxons had gods called *Tiw*, *Woden*, *Thunor* and *Frig* (related to Scandinavian *Tyr*, *Othin*, *Thór* and *Frigg*). Woden was particularly important, shown by the fact that most of the early kings claimed descent from him. He also appears in a number of surviving placenames – Woodnesborough (Kent), Wednesbury and Wednesfield (W Midlands) and Wensley (Derbyshire). Clusters of placenames, such as those referring to his 'barrow', 'valley' and 'dyke' in Wiltshire, point to special sanctuaries dedicated to this god. Wansdyke (OE *wodnes dic*) and similar names suggest that he was thought to assist in building great earthworks. A story about Woden seems to be behind an allusion in an Anglo-Saxon charm against poison:

> *A serpent came gliding and tore a man to bits. Then Woden took nine glory-twigs and struck the snake so that it broke into nine pieces.*

This implies that Woden was famous for his knowledge of protective magic.

Of the others even less is known. Thunor, like Scandinavian Thór, was associated with thunder and lightning. He was famous for his hammer – the thunderbolt – and amulets in this shape have been found in graves at Gilton (Kent). A reference in later Anglo-Saxon literature to thunder thrashing the devil with his fiery axe may preserve a dim memory of Thunor and his traditional weapon. Placenames recording Thunor's name – Thunderfield (W Sussex), and Thundersley (Essex) – are associated in particular with open spaces (*feld*) and clearings (*leah*), which may mean that he was also a fertility god. Little is known of Tiw and Frig, whose names appear in one or two placenames as well as in Tuesday and Friday. The runic letter ↑ is called Tiw after the name of the god, and something resembling it has been found inscribed on a sixth-century sword-pommel from Faversham in Kent. This might mean that *Tiw* was a wargod like Scandinavian Tyr, but there is no other evidence of this.

One or two other names suggest mythological stories. The name *wælcyrge*, usually glossed as 'witch' in surviving Christian literature, literally means 'chooser of the slaughtered', the same as Scandinavian *Valkyrie*. In a recorded charm, bees in a swarm are referred to as *sigewif*, 'victory women', reminiscent of the *Valkyries* riding through the air to battle. *Wyrd*, 'fate', is sometimes personified in Anglo-Saxon poetry and said to weave men's destiny. These and many more references could refer to aspects of an old mythology, but are not susceptible to proof.

PAGAN RELIGION

We know something about pagan religious practices in England, that is, about the organised worship of the deities. In a work called *On Computation of Time*, Bede describes the months of the pre-Christian year and in doing so mentions several of the old religious customs. February was *sol-monath*, which means (according to Bede) 'month of cakes' after the offerings made at this time. March and April were named after two goddesses, *Hreda* and *Eostre* (equivalent to Latin *Aurora*), whose festivals occurred then. September was 'holy month' or 'month of festivities', perhaps comparable to our harvest thanksgiving. November was called *blot-monath*, meaning 'month of sacrifices', 'because in that month they dedicated to their gods the animals they were about to kill'. The first and last months of the year were called *Giuli* (Yule), during which occurred 'the night of mothers', equivalent to our New Year's Eve, which Bede thinks may have taken its name from certain ceremonies held then.

Other evidence of religious activities comes from the Anglo-Saxon charms, in some of which a residue of pagan ritual is to be found, mingled with Christianity. One of the most explicit is a charm for securing fertility of the soil which seems to allude by name to another of the old goddesses. The farmer is advised, among other things, to cut four turves from the four quarters of his land and have a priest sing four masses over them; to take meal of every kind and bake a small loaf kneaded with milk and holy water and to lay it under the first furrow, reiterating a specified incantation; then to buy unknown seed from beggars and, laying it on the plough, to say:

> *Erce, Erce, Erce, mother of earth! May the almighty, the eternal lord, grant you fields growing and flourishing, fruitful and thriving, bright shafts of (?)-crops, and of broad barley-crops, and of white wheat-crops, and of all crops of the earth . . .*

Anglo-Saxon historical writers, who were all Christians, preferred to avoid specific references to pagan deities and their rites, and alluded instead only to such things as 'idols' and 'offerings'. But sometimes more is revealed almost by accident. Such a case occurs in Bede's *Ecclesiastical History* in the description of the conversion of the court of King Edwin of Northumbria to Christianity in 627:

The King publicly gave his permission for Paulinus to preach the Gospel, and, renouncing idolatry, declared that he received the faith of Christ. And when he asked the high priest who should first profane the altars and temples of their idols, with the enclosures that were about them, he answered, 'I. For who can more properly than myself destroy those things which I worshipped through ignorance, as an example to all others, through the wisdom which has been given to me by the true God?' And immediately, out of contempt of his former superstitions, he asked the king to provide him with weapons and a stallion, and mounting the horse he set out to destroy the idols. It was not permitted before for the high priest either to carry arms or to ride on anything other than a mare. So, with sword girt and with spear in hand, he went on the king's stallion to the idols. The crowd, seeing all this, thought that he was mad; but he lost no time, for as soon as he came near the temple he profaned it, throwing into it the spear which he carried; and rejoicing in the knowledge of the worship of the true God, he commanded his companions to destroy the temple with all its enclosures, by fire. This place where the idols were can still be seen, not far from York, to the east beyond the river Derwent, and is now called Godmundingham [modern Good-manham], where the high priest, by the inspiration of the true God, profaned and destroyed the altars which he himself had consecrated.

This account reveals incidentally that there was a hierarchical priesthood observing certain taboos and also centralised places of worship.

Further information about cult centres comes from placenames. The element *hearh*, 'hill sanctuary', occurs in such names as Harrowden (Bedfordshire, Northamptonshire), Arrowfield Top (Hereford and Worcestershire) and Harrow (London), originally recorded as *gumeninga hearh*, 'the sanctuary of the tribe called the *Gumeningas*'. *Weoh* or *wih* in names appears to mean 'idol' or 'shrine', and survives in Weedon (Buckinghamshire, Northamptonshire), Wheeley (Essex) and Willey (Surrey).

FOLKLORE AND SUPERSTITIONS

A third type of paganism might best be called superstitious folklore. Like the ancient Greeks, the Anglo-Saxons believed that mysterious and desolate places were inhabited by creatures whose anger had to be appeased or goodwill secured. The Christians often acknowledged the existence of these beings, believing them to belong to the evil race descended from Cain. Examples of Cain's progeny are the trolls, like Beowulf's opponent, Grendel, and the elves, whose missiles (elf-shot) were thought to pierce their victims' skin, causing disease. Dragons were thought to inhabit old burial mounds, and appear in literature as fire-breathing guardians of hidden treasure. The creatures whom St Guthlac found inhabiting the fens, when he arrived to set up his hermit's cell at Crowland, were

> *ferocious in appearance, terrible in shape, with great heads, long necks, thin faces, yellow complexions, filthy beards, shaggy ears, wild foreheads, fierce eyes, foul mouths, horses' teeth, throats vomiting flames, twisted jaws, thick lips, strident voices, singed hair, fat cheeks, pigeon breasts, scabby thighs, knotty knees, crooked legs, swollen ankles, splay feet, spreading mouths and raucous cries.*

Widespread belief in the existence of such creatures is reflected in placenames like Drakelow (Derbyshire) and Dragley 'dragon's mound' (Lancashire); also Shugborough (Staffordshire), Shucklow (Buckinghamshire) and

Shobrooke (Devon), all containing the word *scucca*, 'spectre'. In old records there are two examples of *grendles mere*, 'Grendel's lake' and one of *grendles pyt*, 'Grendel's pit', suggesting that some people may have regarded the monster described in *Beowulf* as very much a reality.

Fig 18   Pictures of devils in manuscripts

Not all unknown creatures were thought of as evil. Of the two types of giant, *ent* and *thyrs*, the former is sometimes credited in literature with the construction of great buildings. There are several occurrences of *enta geweorc*, 'the work of giants', referring to the remains of Roman building in stone which the Anglo-Saxons admired but could not emulate. There was also a widespread pantheistic belief in powers which inhabited springs, wells, stones and trees. Many names of the type 'holy well' or 'holy tree' may go back to Anglo-Saxon times, and there is a reference in a charter of 854 to an ash tree 'which the ignorant call holy'. A law of Cnut (d 1035) strictly forbids all heathen practices, which it proceeds to describe:

Heathenism is when a man worships idols, that is, when he worships the heathen gods, and the sun or the moon, fire or water, springs or rocks or any kind of tree, or takes

*an interest in witchcraft, or commits murder of any sort
either through sacrifice or through fear, or does any
deluded things such as these.*

The mention of black magic brings to mind the witchcraft
referred to in a charter of 975 which traced the ownership of
an estate then belonging to Wulfstan Ucca. A widow and her
son had previously forfeited the land because she had driven
an iron pin into Ælfsige, Wulfstan's father (presumably into
a model of him), and the crime had been detected. They
dragged the deadly image from her chamber, seized the
woman and drowned her at London Bridge, but her son
escaped to become an outlaw.

Charms and magical rituals were originally passed on
orally, but in Christian times some of them were written
down and two substantial collections survive. Most are in the
form of medicinal recipes with accompanying action.
Though much modified and corrupted by constant recopy-
ing, these show something of the blend of early magic, Christian superstition and classical medical lore which was at the
heart of Anglo-Saxon belief about the natural world and
how it might be kept in order. A fairly typical example is the
following formula for a horse which has become
dangerously distended from overeating green food:

*If a horse is elf-shot, take that knife of which the handle
is made from the fallow horn of an ox and let there be
three brass nails on it. Then inscribe the mark of Christ
on the forehead of the horse so that it bleeds, then inscribe the mark of Christ on its back and on all the limbs
you can. Then take the left ear and pierce it in silence.
This you shall do: take a stick and strike it on the back.
Then it will be cured. And write on the horn of the knife
these words:* Benedicite omnia opera domini dominum.
Whatever elf is involved, this will cure him.

There are several elements here which recur in other charms.
Belief in the darts of wicked creatures is a common feature of
Anglo-Saxon animism, while the blood-letting and striking,
like beating a lunatic or smoking cattle, served to purge the

victim and drive the evil one out. The importance of the cross, the number three and the incantation is also typical.

Driving out the evil influence is known as *antipathetic* magic, but equally common is *sympathetic* magic in which a symbolic action parallels the cure. One charm for curing a swelling is as follows:

> *Take a root of a lily and sprouts of elder-tree and a leaf of garlic. Cut them into very small parts and pound them well. Put them in a thick cloth and bind over the swelling.*

Here the constituent plants in the poultice show in themselves some sort of swelling or thickening, so that chopping and pounding them is efficacious by association. Primitive though the treatment may be, there is often a systematic, logical attitude of mind underlying the medicine-man's antics and mumbo-jumbo.

FUNERAL METHODS

Methods for disposing of the dead consisted of cremation, inhumation, or a mixture of the two. In cremation cemeteries, such as those at Sancton (Humberside), Newark (Nottinghamshire), and Lackford (Suffolk), urns containing the remains were laid out in rows, often over a large area. A study of cremations at Illington (Norfolk) shows that the corpse was laid on the ground and a funeral pyre heaped above it. Fusing of glass beads found among the ashes reveals that a temperature of 900°C was reached. After the fire the bones were gathered into an urn, either specially made for the purpose or, less often, an ordinary cookingpot. Objects such as jewellery, knives, bone playingpieces and combs, either burnt or unburnt, were often buried with the remains, and sometimes unburnt, specially made, miniature implements were included.

Cremation required organisation, time and a good supply of fuel – factors which may account for the popularity of inhumation, the alternative method, which increased as the pagan period progressed. The inhumed body was usually laid extended on its back, in many cases accompanied by gravegoods, such as knives, jewellery, weapons, or vessels of various sorts. There is some evidence of food but burial of whole animals is rare, only skeletons of dogs and horses being discovered complete. Burial with gravegoods was discouraged by the Christian church but did not cease immediately. In a cemetery at Saffron Walden (Essex) items were buried with the dead as late as the tenth or eleventh century. The mixed rite involved partial burning of the corpse which was afterwards inhumed.

Two other methods were barrow- and ship-burial. The first began in the sixth century with interments in old Bronze-Age mounds where they existed in Wiltshire, the Peak District and the Yorkshire Wolds. Later there were primary interments in specially made barrows, like the richly furnished ones at Taplow and Benty Grange (Derbyshire). Ship-burials have been discovered in East Anglia at Sutton Hoo, Snape and Caister-on-Sea.

The ideas behind these customs can only be guessed at. Cremation may have symbolised release of the spirit and the practice of deliberately piercing cremation urns may be connected with this. The extensive burial of gravegoods, on the other hand, seems to be provision for continuing life, although the objects most useful for everyday existence are often disregarded – weapons, for instance, were preferred in men's graves to tools and domestic utensils. Or was life to continue in another world, on the journey to which the East Anglian king would be glad of the ship buried at Sutton Hoo? Whatever the case, we are probably right in suspecting that elaborate rituals were involved. One of the penitentials of Theodore forbids, as superstitious, the practice of burning grain when a man died 'for the health of the living and of the house'. Just such a custom seems to have been observed in cemeteries at Marston (Northamptonshire) and Sandy (Bedfordshire), where quantities of burnt grain were found.

HEROIC IDEALS

To achieve a more coherent impression of the beliefs and

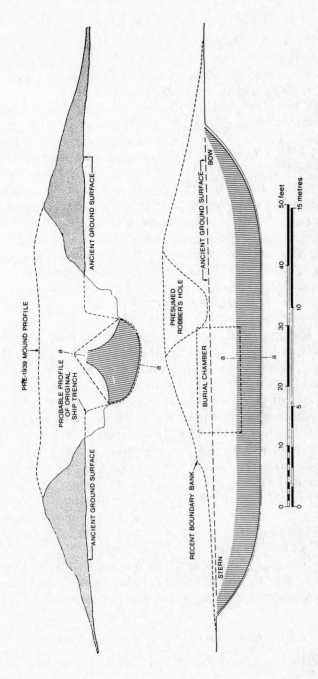

PRE-1939 MOUND PROFILE

ANCIENT GROUND SURFACE

PROBABLE PROFILE
OF ORIGINAL
SHIP TRENCH

ANCIENT GROUND SURFACE

a

a

PRESUMED
ROBBER'S HOLE

ANCIENT GROUND SURFACE

BOW

BURIAL CHAMBER

a

a

RECENT BOUNDARY BANK

STERN

0   10   20   30   40   50 feet

0   5   10   15 metres

Fig 19 Two sections through the ship-barrow at Sutton Hoo
(*The Sutton Hoo Ship Burial: A Handbook*)

ideals of the Anglo-Saxons it is necessary to consider their literature, all of which was written in Christian times. Some of the non-religious material is believed to have its roots in pre-Christian traditions which were passed on by word of mouth. Not all of the early ideals were superseded at conversion, and it is unlikely that church teaching sought to eradicate all the moral standards of former times. The poem *The Battle of Maldon* contains ideas of glory in battle, absolute loyalty to one's lord, and the heroism of defence until death, which thrilled the spirits of warriors in the meadhall in the earliest times, perhaps even in the homelands on the continent of Europe. Christian literature is sometimes affected by the heroic tradition – Jesus is described as a young hero willingly mounting the cross, and in a poem called *Judith* the Old Testament heroine of that name disposes of Holofernes with a spirit that would not have discredited an ancient Germanic champion.

Three of the most important ideals are concerned with fame, loyalty and fate. The suggestion is present, even in works which are strongly Christian in parts, that, as life after death is uncertain, the most a man can do is to take care that his good reputation will survive him. For this reason an heroic stand against overwhelming odds, like that of the hero Waldhere, was one of the most popular themes, not only of English stories but also of stories throughout the Germanic world. A brave defence was often undertaken out of loyalty to a lord or to avenge his death. Sometimes a conflict of loyalties adds tragic depth, as when a warrior, in obedience to his leader, finds himself in the opposite party to his own kinsmen. There is a strong sense of the fatal power which places men in such positions. The lordless outcast of *The Wanderer* laments that 'fate is inexorable ... and the weary-hearted cannot oppose it', while the *Maxims* list the power of fate as one of the inevitable facts of life: 'fate is strongest, winter coldest, spring frostiest ...'

CONVERSION TO CHRISTIANITY

In 597 a Christian mission from Rome, led by Augustine,

landed on the island of Thanet (Kent). King Æthelbert, whose Frankish wife, Bertha, was already a Christian, nevertheless regarded the newcomers with suspicion, receiving them in the open air for fear of sorcery. Within a year, however, the king himself was converted and the conversion of the heathen English had begun.

An attempt by Paulinus, a successor of Augustine, to extend Christian influence into Northumbria, met with initial success when King Edwin was baptised in 627. However, the success was shortlived, for Edwin was killed in the battle of Hatfield Chase in 632, and Paulinus fled, his work of conversion hardly begun. On the death of Cadwallon, the conqueror of Edwin, Oswald succeeded to the kingdom. He had spent the years of Edwin's reign in exile in the north and had come under the influence of Christians from Ireland at the island monastery of Iona (Argyll). Accordingly, on his accession, he requested the abbot of Iona to send him men who might help to re-establish Christianity in Northumbria. A group of monks, led by Aidan, journeyed to Lindisfarne (Northumberland), an island still only accessible by road at low tide. They founded a monastery there in 635 and, with this as their centre, achieved remarkable success in converting the people and setting up other monasteries in the Irish pattern.

Soon a situation arose in which large parts of the country, mainly in the north, followed the teaching of the Celtic missionaries, while converts of Augustine and his successors adhered to the Roman practice. The differences – concerning matters of ecclesiastical organisation, and the computation of the date of Easter – had come about as a result of the independent growth of the Celtic church from the rest of Europe. The situation became intolerable in the Northumbrian court of King Oswy, who is said to have observed Easter at a time when his Kentish queen was still fasting and observing Palm Sunday. It was felt that the conflict must be resolved and to this end a synod was held at Whitby, in 663, at which Wilfrid argued for the Roman practice whilst Colman, bishop of Lindisfarne, acted as opposing spokesman. King Oswy, perhaps appreciating the advantages of increased contacts with Rome, decided that the Celtic usage should be abandoned. Those who disagreed withdrew from Northumbria and the way was open for a concerted effort to unite the country in its new faith.

MISSIONARY ACTIVITY

The response to missionary activity varied throughout the country. Mercia cast off paganism only after 653; Sussex not until 681, and everywhere those who embraced the new faith were in constant danger of relapsing into heathenism. A famous letter from Pope Gregory gives general advice as to how the Roman mission should proceed.

The temples of the idols in that nation ought not to be destroyed, but let the idols that are in them be destroyed and let holy water be made and sprinkled, altars erected and relics deposited. For if those temples are well built it is requisite that they be converted from the worship of devils to the service of the true God, that the people, seeing that their temples are not destroyed may remove error from their hearts, and, knowing and adoring the true God, more familiarly resort to the places to which they have been accustomed.

According to Bede, the East Anglian king, Rædwald, wished for the best of both religions and had two altars in the same temple – one dedicated to Christ and a smaller one at which he offered victims to the devils. Conversion to Christianity did not happen overnight. It was over forty years after Augustine's landing before the Kentish king, Earconbert, felt able to command the destruction of idols throughout his kingdom and to enforce the Lent fast.

Visible monuments to this missionary zeal survive in the form of sculptured stone crosses and churches. The crosses, particularly numerous in the north and north Midlands, were first set up as a clear symbol of Christianity, sanctifying the land for Christian use, whether for worship or burial, and perhaps acting as preaching stations in places where churches did not exist. Later ones were used over individual burials and as boundary marks. Two of the finest crosses, at Ruthwell (Dumfriesshire) and Bewcastle (Cumberland) are also among the earliest. Both are of sandstone, 17 and 14ft (5.1 and 4.2m) high, respectively, as they now stand, and belong to the period soon after the Synod of Whitby when Anglo-Saxon, Irish and Mediterranean styles fused into the

Fig 20

Sculptured stone cross at Ruthwell – height 17ft (W. G. Collingwood, *Northumbrian Crosses*)

distinctive patterns and figures with which the crosses are carved.

The earliest crosses in the north were made of wood, like the one which King Oswald set up on Heavenfield before he overcame Cadwallon, and in this respect were like the earliest northern churches, such as those at York and Lindisfarne. One of the most complete examples of the type of stone church which eventually replaced them can be seen at Escomb, near Bishop Auckland. It is built of stone re-used from the nearby Roman station of Vinovia (Binchester) and has a tall, narrow nave, 43½ft (14m) long, originally lighted only by five, small, splayed windows set high in the walls. Two small doorways give entrance into the nave from outside, and a third into the chancel, which is only 10ft (3m) square. The overall impression is of simple austerity.

Early southern churches were more open in plan. No clear example survives, but the ground plan is best seen at Reculver, Kent. This nave was 37 by 24ft (11 by 7m), divided from the apsidal chancel by a triple arcade in front of which stood a large painted cross. Gradually the first church was augmented with side chambers, towers and other extensions. Only the Norman towers were left standing after its thoughtless demolition in 1805.

MONASTICISM

The church at Escomb was probably a field church, built by a nobleman on his own lands and occupied by a secular priest. The main centres of Christianity, however, were the monasteries, whose main churches (minsters) were grander buildings, like those at Hexham (Northumberland) and St Augustine's, Canterbury. The earliest monasteries in the north of England were built on the Irish pattern and consisted of a number of scattered oratories and dwelling places within an enclosure. There were usually few communal buildings – perhaps no more than a refectory and a church. Later monasteries tended to conform to the Benedictine Rule, but until the tenth century there was a strong tradition of independence. Benedict Biscop, for instance, devised the rule for his own foundations at Monkwearmouth and Jarrow (Tyne and Wear) from those which he had experienced in seventeen monasteries on his travels, and there were numerous double houses, like those of Whitby and Repton, where monks and nuns worked and worshipped in close proximity.

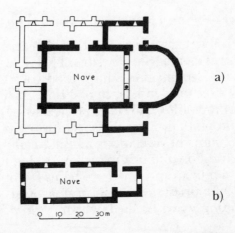

Fig 21   Plans of early churches at (a) Reculver; (b) Escomb

The monasteries were also great evangelising and teaching centres. Bede, as a boy of seven, was entrusted to the care of the brethren at Monkwearmouth and, apart from transferring to the twin foundation at Jarrow, seems to have ventured out very little by the time he died in 735 aged about sixty-two. Despite his immobility, Bede's faith and scholarship reached and inspired others throughout Europe through his books, the result of patient study in the great library assembled by Benedict Biscop. We read that St Cuthbert, in his youth, used to spend months preaching and converting in desolate places, which others feared to approach. The earliest abbots and bishops of the north were also assiduous in these labours and it is often said that they travelled about their extensive dioceses on foot ministering in person to the needs of their flock.

An impression of the life of the novice monk is provided by Ælfric in his *Colloquy*. Every day he sings seven offices with the brethren. He is also greatly occupied in reading and is so anxious to learn that he is willing to be flogged if his teacher thinks it necessary. As a novice he is allowed meat in addition to the normal diet of the monks. He sleeps in the dormitory and is awakened for nocturnes by the bell or by the rod of the novice-master.

CHRISTIAN SUPERSTITIONS

The converted Anglo-Saxons were as credulous in their own way as their pagan ancestors. This is clear from the hold which the demons and superstitions of old continued to exercise over their minds. In addition, their faith in the efficacy of the saints and relics of the new religion was often undiscriminating. Even the sober history of Bede abounds with accounts of revelations and miraculous cures – cattle and men restored to health on consuming the dust from St Chad's tomb; a captive whose chains fell off because of the prayers of a priest; a wooden post, against which St Aidan was leaning when he died, which could not afterwards be

Plate 6 Beginning of the Gospel of St John from the Lindisfarne Gospels (BM MS Cotton Nero D IV). The main Latin text of about AD 700 is in ornamental capitals and reads 'IN PRINCIPIO ERAT UERBUM ET UERBUM ERAT APUD D[EU]M ET D[EU]S . . .' The smaller writing above it is a tenth-century gloss by a scribe named Aldred. It is written in Anglo-Saxon minuscule; the Latin heading is in uncial script. The decoration consists of abstract and animal interlace, predominantly in reds, greens, blues, yellows and purples, against a background of black. Much of the design is outlined with chains of minute red dots, hardly any of which have come loose – a sign of the effectiveness of the eggwhite binding medium. The 'c' of the second line terminates in a man's head. This is the only instance of anthropomorphic decoration in this manuscript, although it became very popular later, for instance in the ninth-century *Book of Kells* (British Library).

Incipit euangelium secundum Iohan

IN PRINCIPIO ERAT UERBUM ET UERBUM ERAT ABUD DM ET DS

burned, and so on. We may suspect that the saints' lives also stole popularity from the old tales, for they were the heroic legends of the new order.

St Guthlac's encounters with horrifying demons have already been touched upon. Even more remarkable is the biography of St Cuthbert. As a shepherd boy he was converted to the service of God in 651 by the sight of St Aidan's soul being borne to Heaven by angels. Many stories are told of his devotion and asceticism. An unsuspected onlooker reported that once, when others were asleep, Cuthbert waded up to his armpits in the cold sea to mortify his flesh while he chanted psalms. Cuthbert eventually moved to Lindisfarne as prior, but attained permission to relinquish his office and withdrew to the desolate Farne Islands where, having expelled the customary evil spirits, he built a hermitage of stones, turf and thatch dug deep into the ground to prevent his gaze from straying upon anything but the heavens. He prayed for, and was granted, a spring of clear water; he reproved the birds who stole his thatch so that they gestured their apology; even the sea responded to his command. So unmindful was he of his physical care that he kept his shoes

Plate 7 Anglo-Saxon church at Barton-on-Humber. The large nave on the east side is a fourteenth-century extension. The original building had only a small eastern annexe, like the one still standing on the west side. The central tower was the largest part of this type of church. It has many classic features. There are characteristic quoins, or cornerstones which match the pilaster strips decorating the tower. The plaster covers typical rubble walls. Double windows, both roundheaded and pointed, can be seen with their mid-wall baluster shafts; there is a plain but noble doorway built all of throughstones. The western annexe, which is not at right angles to the tower, retains the steep pitch of its early roof, but not of course the original materials. Probably built about the beginning of the eleventh century.

on from one Easter to the next, removing them only for the Maundy-Thursday washing of the feet. For nine years he continued in devotional solitude, meeting only those who came to seek his advice and comfort. Eventually he left Inner Farne against his will to become bishop of Lindisfarne, but returned there at the end of 686, to die two months later. Buried on Lindisfarne, his body was removed in 875, when Viking attacks caused the monks to abandon the island, and later transferred to Durham, where the present cathedral was built in his honour.

6

How They Spoke and Wrote

OLD ENGLISH

THE English language up to about 1100 is usually called Old English, to about 1500 Middle English, and thereafter Modern English. Here is an example of written Old English accompanied by a literal gloss:

From the Gospel of St Matthew VII, 24-7

Ælc   þara   þe þas min word gehierþ and þa
Each of them/those who these my words heareth and them

wyrcþ biþ gelic þæm wisan were se his hus   ofer
worketh, is like the wise man who his house on/over

stan getimbrode. þa   com   þær regen and micel flod,
stone built   Then came there rain and much flood,

and þær bleowon windas and ahruron on þæt hus, and hit
and there blew   winds and fell   on the house and it

na ne feoll. Soþlice hit wæs ofer stan getimbrod.
not   fell. Truly   it was on stone built.

   And ælc þara   þe gehierþ þas min word and þa
   And each of those who heareth these my words and them

ne wyrcþ, se biþ gelic þæm dysigan menn þe getimbrode
not worketh, he is like the foolish man who   built

his hus ofer sand-ceosol. þa   rined hit, and þær comon
his house on sand-gravel. Then rained it, and there came

flod,   and   bleowon windas and   ahruron   on þæt hus;
floods, and   blew winds and [they] fell on the   house;

and þæt hus feoll, and his hryre wæs   micel.
and the house fell, and its   fall   was much/great.

To most present day English people this would seem like a foreign language completely unrelated to their own, and it is true that the differences are very striking. There are special symbols, no longer used, the 'þ' for '*th*', and the 'æ' for the vowel sound of modern 'hat' (short) or 'hare' (long). Old English had a much more complex system of word endings (inflexions) by which meaning could be conveyed: Modern English relies rather on word order and the use of prepositions such as 'of', 'by', 'with'. *þara* (line 1) means 'of them' as distinct from *þa* (line 1) which means simply 'them'. *þæm* and *þæt* (2 and 4) both mean 'the', but have different (though related) forms because they refer to different types of words. Similarly *com* and *comon* (3 and 8) both mean 'came', the difference here being that one has a singular subject (rain) and the other a plural subject (floods), a distinction which speakers of English have since found unnecessary. *Flod* and *word* (9 and 1) are plural, though they look singular, because they belong to a type of noun which did not indicate plurality by any ending – like 'sheep' and 'deer' today. There were more such words in Old than in Modern English and comparatively fewer of the type like *windas* (4) where the plural was formed in the regular modern way by the addition of an -*s* ending.

On the other hand, the similarities are almost as striking as the differences. Well over two-thirds of the vocabulary is still in use today, although some words only become recognisable when pronunciation is taken into account. In *regen* (3), for instance, it is helpful to know that the 'g' was pronounced 'y', and in *ofer* (2) that the 'f' was pronounced 'v'. The word *stan* (3) has in Middle English been subject to a change of sound which linguists call 'rounding', in which the speaker rounds his lips when pronouncing the vowel, producing in this case 'stone'. This is a consistent sound change and affects *an*, 'one'; *ban*, 'bone'; *mara*, 'more', and so on. Once the pattern is recognised this type of change is comprehensible and presents no difficulty. Other words have undergone change of meaning, like *wyrcþ*(2), which is recognisable as 'worketh', but here means 'does, performs'. *Soþlice* (5) is simply 'sooth+ly', and *were* (2) 'man' is recognisable in the compound *werewolf* ('man+wolf'). *Micel* (3) occurs in placenames such as Michelmarsh (Hampshire). *Ceosol*(8), 'gravel', is preserved in Chiselborough (Somerset) and Chesil Bank (Dorset).

The sounds of Old English can be tentatively reconstructed by a process of detective work, using spellings, loan-words, comparison with other related languages, and by considering the subsequent development of words up to the present day.

DIALECTS

Old English was made up of a number of dialects which were more marked than the dialects of present-day English. Dialects come about when a speech community is geographically or socially separated, so that each of the parts develops differently. It would be impossible to say exactly how many dialects there were. Even if we had adequate written evidence for all areas, which we have not, there would be no means of understanding the complexities of spoken Old English – comprehension between dialect groups, and so on. However, from surviving records, four main ones are usually distinguished – West Saxon, Kentish, Mercian, and Northumbrian, corresponding approximately to the four major kingdoms.

However, Scandinavian influence, especially the settlement of large numbers of Danes and Norwegians in the north and east, was a complicating factor. The effects of their languages can be appreciated from the fact that East and West Mercian developed into substantially different dialects of Middle English. Today, areas of Scandinavian influence, such as the Lake District, can be detected most easily from placenames ending in *-by* 'village', *-thwaite* 'clearing, meadow', and *-toft*, 'house-site, homestead'. Words and patterns of speech in the present-day dialects of these areas can often be traced back to Old Danish or Old Norse. But Scandinavian settlement also affected the language more generally, and it has left its mark on what is now regarded as normal English. Few people realise when they use such everyday words as 'call, egg, fellow, hit, husband, ill, low, odd, root, skin, sky, take, they, their, them, ugly, want' and 'wrong' that they are in the debt of the Scandinavian settlers of Anglo-Saxon times from whom these words were borrowed.

We know most about the West Saxon dialect of Old English because the vast majority of surviving literature and documents are written in it. This is because West Saxon became the standard literary and administrative language in late Anglo-Saxon times. But the variety of English which has gained acceptance today does not stem from this source, for West Saxon fell out of favour after the Norman Conquest when for a time no English dialect had particular prestige. Then, in the fourteenth century, when London had acquired commercial, political and social pre-eminence, the dialect of the capital, which by that time had become mainly East Midland, gradually became accepted as the standard form of English, and so subsequently developed, though with many modifications, into the language of today.

WRITING

Pre-Christian Anglo-Saxons were not entirely illiterate. A small number of them knew 'runic' writing – the use of an alphabet of predominantly straight-line letters – for inscriptions on stone, bone, wood and metal. Nearly all surviving inscriptions, however, are post-Conversion. The number and shape of the letters varied from place to place and time to time. In Scandinavia, in the eighth century, systems of only sixteen letters were used, whereas in ninth-century Northumbria the number was as many as thirty-three.

Most inscriptions are simple, brief statements, many of them incomplete or indecipherable. Some fuller ones are of the type 'pray for Cynibalth Cuthber ...' found on a cross

Fig 22   The runic alphabet

fragment at Lancaster, and 'Gilsuith set up this monument to Berhtsuith on her tomb; pray for her soul' on a fragment at Thornhill (W Yorkshire). The longest and most interesting of all are the runes of the Ruthwell Cross, which give a version of an Old English poem, and those carved on the Franks Casket. In addition, some coins have the names of kings in runes.

Christian missionaries introduced the Roman alphabet which superseded the runic. It was in a form developed in Ireland and conveyed to England through the missionaries in the north. The fundamental differences between this and our own alphabet are that 'k', 'q' and 'z' were rarely used, and 'j', 'v' and 'w' not at all. The digraph æ was a vowel, called by its runic name 'ash'. and stood for a sound bwtween 'a' and 'e'. Two symbols were used to express 'th', a 'crossed d' or 'eth' (ð), and the borrowed rune called 'thorn' (þ). Another borrowed rune called wynn, 'joy', was used for 'w', but this is usually modernised in present-day printed texts because of its confusing similarity to þ.

The earliest handwriting is known as 'uncial' and 'half-uncial', the rounded bookhand used for the Latin text of the *Lindisfarne Gospels* and for the *Gospels of St Chad* at Lichfield. The script which developed later and is used in most books of the period is a 'minuscule' script used for the tenth-century English gloss of the *Lindisfarne Gospels* and for the *Cædmon Manuscript* of Old English poetry of approximately the same date. Towards the end of the period, particularly for Latin texts, an elegant French-inspired hand called 'Carolingian minuscule' came into use, seen in the *Benedictional of St Æthelwold*.

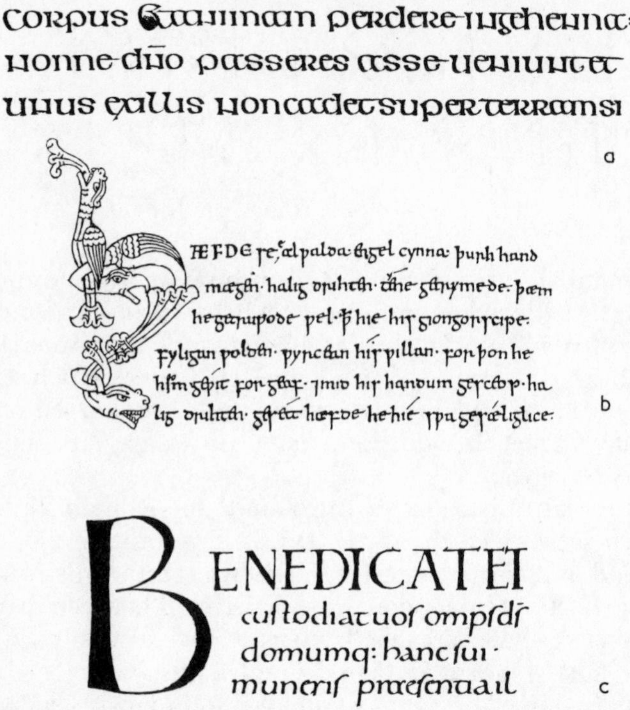

corpus Getaninain perdere iugehenna·
nonne dūo passeres asse ueniunt·
unus galis noncadet super terams·

a

ÆFDE re, ælpaloa·engel cynna· þurh hand
mægen·halig oruhten·ðne geðrymede·þæm
hegerupode pel·þ hie hir giongonrcipe·
fyligan poloen·þynctan hir pillan·for þon he
hlsrn geþic for gær·imuo hir handum gercðp·ha
lig oruhten·geðæ hæfoe·hehie·rpa geræliglice·

b

ENEDICATEI
custodiat uos omprsdi
domumq: hanc sui·
muncris præsentail

c

Fig 23   Examples of Anglo-Saxon scripts: (a) Gospels of St Chad;
(b) 'Cædmon' manuscript; (c) Benedictional of St Æthelwold

BOOKMAKING

With Christianity there also came knowledge of the complex technology of bookmaking. Only a small number of
Anglo-Saxon books have survived the centuries of neglect,
damage and deliberate destruction, but those which remain
show that much artistry and skill went into them. To begin
with, vellum or parchment had to be prepared from the skins
of calves, sheep or goats, which were put through various
processes of soaking in lime-water, depilating, washing,
'fleshing' (removing surplus flesh or fat), stretching and
shaving-down to the required thickness. The sheets were
gathered into booklets, usually of sixteen pages, and then
trimmed, care being taken to have the 'hair' side of the

vellum, which was slightly darker, facing another hair side, and two 'flesh' sides likewise.

Margin and guide lines were made by pricking through several pages at regular intervals and ruling between the marks. Ink was made by one of two methods, involving either a mixture of soot, gum and water, or gallic acid, iron sulphate and gum. The writing instrument was a quill or reed-pen which the scribe kept sharpened with his penknife. The fine illuminated manuscripts involved a whole range of additional processes. Designs had to be planned, using compasses in the case of the *Lindisfarne Gospels*, and outlines inked in. Pigments had to be prepared either by grinding substances such as lapis lazuli and malachite, or by extracting dyes from plants; they were applied with a durable medium which would not discolour with age.

The pages of the *New Minster Charter*, made at Winchester in the tenth century, were stained purple and covered with gold lettering. Gilding came increasingly into use in the tenth century. Then there was the binding, an art in itself, even when it did not involve the setting of gems and precious metalwork with which the most sumptuous books were adorned.

EDUCATION

It was natural, since these arts were introduced by the church, that they should be developed and perfected in Christian institutions such as the monasteries. Not only bookmaking, but the whole range of formal education quickly became the province of the church. Schools were set up to prepare young men for the priesthood by providing organised instruction in interpreting the scriptures, the sciences which regulated the ecclesiastical calendar, religious music, and the metrical rules of religious poetry. Novices were entrusted to the monasteries at an early age, and Ælfric's *Colloquy* gives a sample of one of their Latin lessons. Only in monasteries and schools did those gifted in learning have access to libraries and the chance of contact with other scholars.

A development important for the subsequent history of English was the impetus given to vernacular (as opposed to Latin) studies by King Alfred in the ninth century. Alfred's plan, though implemented through the church, was revolutionary in its organisation and scope.

> *It appears better to me, if you agree* [he wrote to his bishops] *that we . . . should translate those books which it is most necessary for all men to know into that language which we all can understand, and bring it about, as we very easily can with God's help if we have sufficient peace, that all the young sons of freemen now in England who have wealth enough to apply themselves to it, be set to learning so long as they are not able to do any other occupation, until the time when they know how to read English writing well. Afterwards let those whom one would wish to learn further and be promoted to the ecclesiastical order, go on to receive tuition in Latin.*

Though Alfred's later years were not blessed with the necessary peace, the ideal of a centrally inspired scheme of education for any young freeborn man wishing to receive it was, for its day, remarkably enlightened.

POETRY

The Anglo-Saxons had a flourishing literature in both poetry and prose, of which the poetic tradition was the more ancient. The earliest poems of pagan times were not written down, but passed on orally. These dealt with subjects which had been popular and traditional amongst the ancestors of the English, and some of them probably told of myths, legends and historical events, such as the conquest of Britain. In Christian times some of the old poems were written down, much changed, no doubt, from the time when they were first current, but the vast majority were never committed to writing, and have passed out of memory. Only a fraction of those which were set down has survived to the present day, the majority being found in four manuscripts dating from the late tenth or early eleventh centuries. Just how much chance is involved in the survival of Old English manuscripts is shown by the fact that in 1860, at Copenhagen, two fragments of a poem about a hero called Waldere were found in use as part of the binding of a book. It is only by extreme good fortune that the story of Waldere can be reconstructed from a te 1th-century Latin poem on the subject, written by a monk in Switzerland. Medieval records are full of tantalising allusions to stories, like that of Waldere, which are now lost for ever.

Old English poetry was predominantly alliterative. End-rhyme did not become a common feature of English verse until it was introduced from France after the Norman Conquest. The basic unit of verse was the half-line, separated from its corresponding half by a natural pause. The two halves were linked together by means of alliteration, which always fell on the strongly stressed syllables, the unstressed syllables in between being variable in number. In the following example from *The Battle of Maldon* the stressed syllables and the central pauses have been marked:

Wódon þa wǽlwulfas, // for wǽtere ne múrnon,
wícinga wérod, // west ofer Pántan,
ofer scír wǽter // scýldas wégon,
lídmen to lánde // linde bǽron.

Advanced (waded) the slaughter-wolves, for water they did
*   not care (mourn),*
troop of Vikings, west over Blackwater,
over clear water shields they carried,
seamen to land bucklers bore.

A literal translation loses some of the alliteration, but the rhythmical structure of this type of verse should be familiar from nursery rhymes like,

Péter Péter Púmpkin Éater
hád a wífe but cóuldn't kéep her.
So he pút her in a púmpkin shéll,
and thére he képt her véry wéll.

Works were declaimed or recited to the accompaniment of harp or lyre and therefore might as accurately be termed 'songs' as 'poems'.

Surviving poetry can be roughly categorised as heroic, religious, elegiac and gnomic, although few poems belong rigidly to one category only. By chance it happens that one heroic poem, called *Beowulf,* survives in its entirety. Its 3,000 lines tell a fantastic folktale set in a vaguely historical context. It was composed about 700 and relates the deeds of Beowulf, a champion of the southern Swedish tribe of the Geats. Beowulf sails to Denmark to help King Hrothgar whose royal hall has been ravaged by a man-eating monster, Grendel. Beowulf lies in wait, grapples with Grendel, and wrenches off his arm, leaving him to creep back to his lair to die. The entertainment and treasure-giving with which the feat is celebrated give us a glimpse of the aristocratic ideal of warrior-companionship in the meadhall. But the joy is short-lived, for the mother of Grendel comes seeking vengeance and carries off the king's best thane. Beowulf seeks out her underwater cave and destroys her there after a mighty struggle. The hero returns home, and some time later becomes king of the Geats. He reigns for fifty years until he is called upon to save his people from a fire-breathing dragon, in destroying which he sustains a mortal wound. At the end of the poem he is described as 'the mildest of men, the kindest, most gentle to his people and most eager for praise'.

Christian poetry is much more extensive than secular heroic verse. The main subjects are Old Testament paraphrases and narratives, poetical homilies, poems on the lives of Christ, the apostles and saints, and moral allegories based on the supposed habits of animals. Whatever the true origins of Christian poetry in English, a tradition told by Bede ascribes it to an old man called Cædmon, a herdsman at the monastery of Whitby under the rule of the Abbess Hild (d 680). Cædmon had never learnt the art of song and, when the harp was passed around after the communal feast, he would slip away, ashamed, as his turn came near.

On one occasion, when he had crept out and settled himself down in the cattleshed which housed the animals in his charge, someone appeared to him in his sleep saying, 'Cædmon, sing me something'. He replied, 'I don't know how to sing, and for this reason I left the feast and came away here'. But the one who was there said, 'Nevertheless, you can sing for me', and he asked, 'What must I sing?' The other replied, 'Sing to me the Creation'. Cædmon immediately began to sing, in praise of God the Creator, verses which he had never heard before. Once awake he remembered all he had sung in his sleep and added more words in the same style. He became a monk at Whitby and continued to exercise his divine gift of poetry.

The *Hymn* which Cædmon received in his dream has survived and is probably the earliest extant poem in English:

Now we must praise the keeper of the heavenly kingdom, the might of the Creator and the thoughts of his mind, the work of the glorious Father as He, the eternal Lord, established the beginning of every wonder. The holy Creator first made heaven as a roof for the sons of men [or children of earth]. After that, the Guardian of mankind, the eternal Lord and almighty Ruler, made for men a middle-enclosure, the earth.

It is difficult to see why so simple a poem was considered remarkable. Probably it was because here, for the first time, Christian subject matter was expressed in traditional alliterative verse.

A small group of poems known as elegies stands midway between the Christian and heroic traditions. Their theme is the transitory nature of human life. They tell longingly of past conviviality in the meadhall, of treasure-giving, of music and friendship, and contrast these with present exile, bereavement, poverty, cold and hardship at sea. In these poems God's mercy and divine Providence are glorified as the sole remedy for harsh misfortunes, but some heroic ideals such as stoicism and good reputation are also adhered to. Among the best are *The Wanderer, The Seafarer* and *Deor's Lament*, the last an interesting stanzaic piece in which a poet, who has fallen from favour, comforts himself by recounting past hardships which were overcome. The poem begins with a reference to the legend depicted on the left-hand front panel of the Franks Casket (Plate 2):

Wayland, resolute warrior, suffered hardships, experienced exile. He had grief and longing as his companions, winter-cold banishment. Often he found sorrow after Nithhad enslaved him and put supple bonds of sinew upon a better man than himself. That passed away, and so may this.

The last group of poems can for convenience be called 'gnomic' that is, consisting of maxims or wise and sententious sayings. First, there are the true *Gnomic Verses* or *Maxims*, which express moral precepts and commonplace facts. These occasionally rise to the level of poetry, but are more interesting for the light they shed on Anglo-Saxon ideas and customs. Then there is a small collection of *Proverbs*, which contain an occasional glimmer of humour: 'Those do not quarrel who are not together.'

The Fates of Men consists of a catalogue of good and evil fortunes which may come upon a man during his lifetime, with most emphasis on the gloomier prospects:

One shall pass through life blinded, grope with his hands. Another, lame in foot, sick with damaged sinews, shall lament his pain.

Its companion-piece *The Arts of Men* surveys more cheerfully the talents with which men are endowed and reflects on God's bounty. *The Runic Poem* gives the names of twenty-nine runes with descriptions of the objects to which they refer. Thus

ᚻ *(hail) is the whitest of grains: it falls from the clouds of heaven, gusts of wind whirl it about, then it turns into water.*

Yet another is *The Dialogue of Salomon and Saturn*, cast as a battle of wits between Salomon, representing Christianity, and Saturn, representing oriental and Germanic paganism. All of these, with the riddles and charms mentioned elsewhere in this book, constitute the bulk of extant Anglo-Saxon poetry.

PROSE

Prose literature may have had its roots in a saga tradition passed on orally, but the earliest written prose was in Latin. Chronicles, histories, saints' lives and epistles were among the most common genres, and the great exponents were Aldhelm (d 709), Bede (d 735) and Alcuin (d 804). Most of the earliest surviving vernacular prose was instigated by King Alfred, both in the translations which he had made and in the *Anglo-Saxon Chronicle*, probably begun under his influence. The works he chose for translation were Gregory's *Cura Pastoralis*, 'Pastoral Care', which set out guidelines for the higher clergy; Orosius's *History*, the standard historical geography book of the time; Bede's *Ecclesiastical History*, the classic account of the Christianisation of England; Boethius's *Consolation of Philosophy*, one of the most popular of all books in the Middle Ages, and St Augustine of Hippo's *Soliloquies*, a meditative work concerned with the eternal life of the soul. Thereafter these works were extensively copied and recopied.

Though Alfred's translations were full and lively and the original prose frequently vigorous and moving, their style is underdeveloped in comparison to works by the later exponents, Wulfstan (d 1023) and Ælfric (d 1020). Wulfstan, who became archbishop of York in 1002, was active in the field of law and administration, but is most remembered for his thundering sermons denouncing the slide into sin and despair which accompanied the renewed Scandinavian attacks of the early eleventh century. Using a prose which, in its rhythms and alliteration, had something in common with Old English poetry, he painted the blackest picture of contemporary life in his *Address to the English*:

Here are manslaughterers and slayers of kinsmen, murderers of priests and haters of churches, and here are perjurors and bringers of death, and here are prostitutes and infanticides and many foul fornicating adulterers,

*and here are sorcerers and witches, and here are robbers,
rapists and thieves, and, in short, a countless number of
crimes and misdeeds of all sorts.*

Ælfric is known as a teacher in Latin and English, most
famous for his homilies, saints' lives, and biblical
translations. As a grammarian he was keenly interested in all
aspects of language and his mature prose is usually regarded
as classical Old English.

Plate 8 Boar-crested helmet from Benty Grange, found in a
seventh-century barrow in Derbyshire, presumably a chieftain's. The plates of horn which once covered the iron frame
have rotted away, but one of the ridges of rust which formed
between them before they disappeared can be seen running up
the nearest band. The projecting lumps are the heads of the
silver rivets by which they were fixed. The downward extension on the right shows that the horn plates extended to form a
neckguard; that on the left is a nasal guard decorated with a
silver cross. The 3½in boar is made of bronze, iron and silver,
with gold and garnet eyes. Originally there was a crest along
its back and a tail. It has been wrongly designed, with two
pairs of 'front' legs, the rear ones bending forwards instead of
backwards. This is the only helmet in the whole of the Germanic world with a boar crest, and of two helmets known from
Anglo-Saxon England, is probably the one which is native-
made (Sheffield City Museum).

65

7

How They Fought

THE usual weapons of attack were spear, bow, knife (or *seax*), axe and sword; and of defence, shield, mailshirt and helmet. Most of these can be demonstrated from archaeological evidence, because weapons were often buried in pagan graves, and also sometimes occur as stray finds from the Christian period.

The commonest weapon was the spear which was used for hunting as well as fighting. Unlike the sword, which was an

Plate 9 Bayeux Tapestry. English shieldwall resisting Norman attack at Hastings. This takes place at an early stage in the battle, but shows the pattern of events which persisted throughout – concerted cavalry action on the one side, and stubborn defensive tactics on the other. The archer here is English, and his bow is of the short, not the long type. Bowmen were more used by Duke William, but their arrows proved ineffective against the disciplined hedge of shields. The two-handed battle-axe used by the English is seen in action here, as well as a mace – flying through the air – swords, lances and spears. Some of the Englishmen hold bundles of spears for use as missiles. Chainmail is depicted conventionally by rings or diagonal lines. Characteristic kite-shaped shields are in evidence everywhere on the tapestry, the traditional round shields having fallen out of fashion (Phaidon Press Ltd).

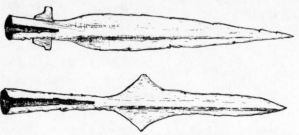

Fig 24   Typical spearheads

aristocratic weapon, the spear was used by all ranks. It was plainly but soundly made, with a leaf-shaped head of hammered iron, the split socket of which was riveted to an ash shaft about 6½ft (2m) long; sometimes it had a pointed, metal ferrule at the other end, by means of which the weapon could be stuck upright into the ground. Heads varied in length from about 2½ to about 24in (7-60cm), and usually had a median rib tapering to the point. Later spearheads were also supplied with side-projections on the socket to prevent the blade from sinking too deep. A thrusting spear known as the *angon* is sometimes found in the south and east of England. This had a barbed head and a length of iron shaft to prevent the head from being hacked off if it became lodged, for instance, in an opponent's shield.

No bow has ever been found intact. At Chessel Down cemetery (Isle of Wight), the excavator thought he could detect the decomposed wood of a bow about 5ft (1.5m) long. The same cemetery, and others, produced arrowheads, some with sockets, like small spearheads, and some with tangs. Despite the lack of archaeological trace, there can be no doubt that the Anglo-Saxons often used bows. An archer named Egil is shown defending himself with bow and arrow on the lid of the Franks Casket. Carved stone crosses often show a bowman-hunter amongst branches of vine. Manuscripts and the Bayeux Tapestry depict archers, and they are also referred to in Old English literature where a bow is the subject of one of the Anglo-Saxon riddles. The type shown in pictures is invariably a short bow.

Knives in graves may be either weapons or domestic utensils, for they are found with women and children as well as warriors. Size is not an infallible distinguishing factor since small ones have been discovered in sheaths attached to the scabbards of swords. The most characteristic form of the weapon, however, is that of the heavy *scramasax*, a broad-bladed, single-edged, hacking weapon of iron with an angled back which slopes in a straight line towards the point. The tang, which is usually without a pommel, is sometimes long enough for the weapon to have been wielded with both hands. Longer and more slender was the so-called *langsax*, of which the best known example is one which was dredged from the river Thames. It is 28in (71cm) in length and has an inlay of bronze and silver along the back of its blade, as well as the complete runic alphabet in silver letters. Most *seaxes*, however, are plain, unpretentious, but useful, weapons. Beowulf's troll-adversary wore one, and the hero himself had one in a sheath attached to his coat of mail.

The axe also was both weapon and tool, but in this case one or two distinct weapon types can be distinguished. One is the throwing axe, or *fransisca*, so called because of its popularity among the Franks. This had a hammered iron head which curved upwards from a short handle to a wide blade – a shape designed to facilitate its use as a missile. There was probably a second type which, like the *angon*, had a length of iron shaft. An axe from Sutton Hoo, 30in (76cm) long, is made entirely of iron. Pictures in manuscripts and in the Bayeux Tapestry show that a huge, heavy axe, of a type introduced by the Danes, was used in hand-to-hand fighting later in the period. T-axes, however, in which a rearward projection from the head functions as a hammer, were probably never used in battle.

Swords were treasured aristocratic weapons, but com-paratively few of them have survived, for they were seldom buried in graves. Literature and various documents show that swords were treated as heirlooms and handed down from father to son. In the eleventh century, Prince Æthelstan bequeathed to his brother a sword which had been owned by the eighth-century king, Offa. In heroic stories they are often given names, such as *Nægling* and

Hrunting in *Beowulf,* a custom which emphasises the close personal feeling a man had for his sword. They might also be lavishly decorated, especially on the hilt.

Surviving swords are mainly double-edged, straight-sided weapons, not sharply pointed, and therefore suited for cutting rather than thrusting. Blade and hilt measure rather less than 3ft (90cm) overall. The blade was sometimes 'pattern-welded' – that is forged and reforged from a bundle of iron rods twisted and beaten to form a flexible core to which a hard, untwisted edge was added. The herring-bone pattern this produced was a sought-after feature, and may have been accentuated by tracing over the blade with acid. A number of epithets for swords in *Beowulf,* such as 'ring-patterned', 'woven-', 'twisted-' and 'shadow-marked', seem to refer to this. The sword was usually worn on the left hip, supported by a baldric in a sheath made of thin laths of wood covered with leather. This was sometimes decorated, for example with appliqué panels, and reinforced at the mouth with a metal band and at the tip with a metal 'chape'.

Swords of the pagan period did not often have pattern-welded blades and usually survive without guard and grip, which suggests that these parts were made of some perishable material. A well preserved hilt from Cumberland (now in the British Museum) is made of horn.

A more serviceable type of sword had developed by the ninth century. The blade was invariably pattern-welded and characteristically had a groove along the length of each side. Its large metal pommel provided counterpoise to the blade, its grip was sometimes bound or plated with metal, and it had a strong metal guard, straight or curved. Fashions in hilt-ornament also changed over the years. In the late sixth century in Kent it became fashionable to decorate the hilts of fine swords with free-running rings and fixed ring-knobs. In the seventh century, gold filigree and garnets were sometimes used. Silver fittings inlaid with *niello* are more characteristic of later swords, a fine example being the all-silver sword-hilt from Fetter Lane in London.

Front

Back

Guara   Repeated

Fig 25   Silver sword hilt
from Fetter Lane, par-
tially   reconstructed –
length   5¾in   (British
Museum – *Guide   to
Anglo-Saxon   An-
tiquities in the BM*)

ARMOUR

Shields were the most common weapons of defence. Their
main component was a wooden board (or 'orb') probably
made of limewood (hence the Old English word for 'shield'
which is *lind*). Over a hole near the centre was fixed a hollow
iron boss, into which the user's knucles fitted as he grasped
the metal bar across its back. The shape of the orb was
usually circular, but by the end of the period other types had
developed. In the Bayeux Tapestry the most common is the
kite-shaped shield, which, being narrow at the base, was
especially suited for use by horsemen. The Tapestry also
shows clearly the leather straps by which the arm was held
close against the shield back, the emblems which were
sometimes painted on the front, and the way in which, at sea,
overlapped shields were fixed along the gunwales of ships.
The boss was most often beaten out of a lump of iron, the
apex of which was worked into a point or 'button'. It was
attached to the orb by means of rivets passing through a
flange – as through the rim of a bowler-hat. The length of

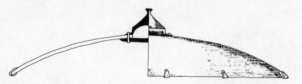

Fig 26   Diagrammatic section of a round shield

the rivets suggest that shields were often little over ½in (1cm) thick, but they could be up to 1½in (3cm), like one from Caenby (Lincolnshire).

Wooden fragments from Petersfinger (Wiltshire) belong to an orb which was laminated like plywood for greater strength. Pictures suggest that round shields were often curved like a watchglass. Their overall diameter is shown, from the few instances where metal rim-fittings occurred, to have been up to about 36in (90cm). The orbs of some shields were decorated with appliqué gilt-bronze panels, geometrical in outline, or in the shape of birds and fishes, and most were probably covered with leather. The laws of Athelstan prescribe a fine of thirty shillings for a shield-maker found to be using leather of an inferior grade. Ordinary men probably had very simple shields, perhaps without any metal fittings whatsoever, and it may be that those which survive are only the grandest. Richest of all is the royal shield from the Sutton Hoo ship-burial, although this was probably not made in England but brought as an heirloom from Sweden.

The Sutton Hoo burial also produced the only surviving example of chainmail. It had been folded when buried and was badly corroded, but radiography shows that the rows of rings were alternately riveted and welded. It was in too poor a condition for the shape of the garment to be recovered. The relative absence of mail is surprising in view of the many references to it in literature. On the Franks Casket, long-sleeved shirts, seemingly of mail, are represented by small, round pellets. The plain battle-garments shown in the same scene may be jerkins and leggings of leather, which presumably afforded protection to the less wealthy. The Bayeux Tapestry, however, gives the most detailed evidence of mail worn in later Saxon times. It is extensively worn by both English and Normans, consisting of a garment comparable in shape to a pair of knee-length combinations, but with legs like a divided skirt so that it might be put on and pulled off over the head.

Not only the shield, but also the sword and helmet from Sutton Hoo are almost certainly Swedish-made. This means that the only surviving Anglo-Saxon helmet is the one discovered in a chieftain's burialmound at Benty Grange in Derbyshire (now in the Sheffield Museum). The Benty Grange helmet (Plate 8) is quite distinct from those of Swedish style in having the crown covered with horn rather than iron. When complete it consisted of a framework of iron bands, some 1in (2.5cm) wide, radiating from the centre of the crown and riveted to a circular iron browband. The eight spaces formed in this way were covered with eight plates of horn, fixed by ornamental silver rivets. The nape-to-nose band of the frame extended downwards at the front to form a nasal which bore a 1½in (4cm) silver cross.

The most striking feature was a free-standing boar about 3½in (9cm) long, set on a bronze plate at the crown of the helmet. It probably was once covered with iron dotted with silver-gilt studs representing bristles, and with silver-gilt plates on the flanks. Its lowered head has blood-red garnet eyes set *en cabochon* in gold filigree sockets, bronze ears and inlaid bronze tusks and muzzle, all of which were gilded. This is a unique example of a free-standing boar-crest, a feature depicted in Celtic and Scandinavian art and mentioned in Germanic literature. In *Beowulf* for instance:

> *The blood-stained sword with its mighty*
> *blade cuts off the boar-images of enemies'*
> *helmets.*

Whatever the religious associations of the boar, it probably symbolised strength, ferocity and willingness to fight. It is interesting that trust in Christ is symbolised by the cross. The occurrence together of the two symbols, one Christian, the other essentially pre-Christian, is in keeping with its seventh-century date.

ENEMIES

It was as fighting men that the Anglo-Saxons first came to England, initially as the mercenaries of the Romans and, later, of the Britons. Under the Romans they were employed against the pirate bands of their own race; under the Britons against the Picts. The story of their revolt against their British employers and of the stubborn resistance they encountered has already been told (Chapter 1). Even when military supremacy had been won by the English, the Britons were still a force to be reckoned with. For instance, in 632 Cadwallon, King of Gwynedd, in alliance with the Mercians, killed the powerful Christian king, Edwin, and overran the whole of his Northumbrian kingdom. Welsh war poetry of the period shows the same fighting spirit as the English.

When they were not engaged against a foreign enemy, the Anglo-Saxon kings occupied themselves in fighting their neighbours for territorial gain, political advantage, or motives of vengeance. In this way the weakest disappeared and the strongest jostled for power. Kent under Æthelbert (d 616), the first Christian king; Northumbria under Edwin, Oswald and Oswy (d 632, 641, 670); Mercia under Offa (d 796), and Wessex under Ecgbert (d 839) all achieved a passing pre-eminence. But in the end the struggle was determined largely by an unexpected outside force – the Vikings.

THE VIKINGS

The Vikings who came were mainly Danes and Norwegians. The Norwegians directed most of their attention to the north-west of England, Wales, Ireland and the Scottish islands; the Danes mainly to the eastern and southern coastal areas of England. The Norwegians were therefore less of a threat to the main centres of government than the Danes. They were motivated by a variety of aims. Their first attacks were sporadic piratical raids probably undertaken with a view to quick gain. Among the earliest targets were exposed monasteries like Lindisfarne which was sacked in 793, a year of terrible portents when there were 'exceptional flashes of lightening, and fiery dragons were seen flying through the air'. A second phase came about the middle of the ninth century, when the intention of many of the invaders became conquest and settlement. This they achieved over large parts of England, but in the tenth century military and political power was wrested from them by the kings of Wessex. The weakness of King Æthelred 'the Unready' and disaffection within his kingdom was an encouragement to the Danes to begin a third phase of raids. A sad period of indecisive leadership and attempts to buy off the attackers led to the accession of Swein and afterwards Cnut, the first Danish kings of all England.

Certainly the Vikings could be vicious and ruthless opponents. Their tactics in war were often more effectual than glorious – refusing to be drawn to open fight, breaking treaties and oaths, needlessly slaughtering civilians. In 1012 when the archbishop of Canterbury refused to pay them tribute money they became incensed and pelted him to death with bones and the heads of cattle. But it would be wrong to over-emphasise their brutality. Some placenames suggest that where they settled they did not automatically deprive English farmers of the best land, but set to work to bring marginal or waste land into cultivation. Their own system of law was well developed, and indeed it was the Scandinavians who first introduced the modern word 'law' into the English language: the Old English word was *æ(w)* 'legal right'. In the sphere of law the Danes collaborated with the English kings. For instance, it was agreed by a treaty circa 886 that in the Danish kingdom of East Anglia there should be no discrimination in *wergilds* to the advantage of Scandinavians over English. Furthermore, Cnut, though not an exemplary Christian in many respects, proved to be a staunch defender of the faith and a benefactor of many religious houses.

TACTICS AGAINST THE DANES

The most graphic account is given in the *Anglo-Saxon Chronicle*. Begun about 890, the *Chronicle* gives a year by year account of national and regional events, as seen from the West Saxon point of view. Contemporary descriptions of Alfred's wars with the Danes are among the fullest entries, and a selection of them is quoted below as the best means of illustrating the military tactics and personal courage which were decisive at that crucial point when England was only narrowly prevented from coming under pagan Scandinavian rule.

Regular mention of marauding Danish armies begins in the Chronicle about the year 832 (real date 835), when for fifteen years they harried the British coast in small numbers (twice said to be thirty-five ships' companies of men). A change of tactics took place in 850/1 when the Danes did not return home before the cold season, but wintered in England and stormed Canterbury and London from a force of 350 ships. In the autumn of 865 an even greater force arrived, a formidable army, which within four years had overcome the Northumbrians and East Anglians and forced the Mercians to make peace. It then turned its attention to Wessex. We take the story in the *Chronicle* from the first year of Alfred's reign:

871   After Easter King Æthelred died, having reigned five years; and his body lies at Wimborne. Then his brother Alfred, son of Æthelwulf, came to the throne of Wessex. And one month later King Alfred fought at the head of a small force against the whole Danish army at Wilton, and was winning for much of the day, but the Danes eventually won possession of the battlefield. And this year nine pitched battles were fought against the Danes in the kingdom south of the Thames, besides those expeditions which Alfred . . . and a single ealdorman and king's thanes often rode on, which no one kept count of; and during the year nine Danish noblemen and one king were killed. And this year the West Saxons made peace with the Danes . . .

878 In midwinter of this year after Twelfth Night the Danish army went secretly to Chippenham, and rode through Wessex and occupied it. A large part of the people was driven oversea and the greatest part of the others was overcome and reduced to submission, except for Alfred the king; and he and a small band of men moved with great difficulty through woods and into hideouts in the marshes . . .

And after Easter King Alfred with a small following built a fort at Athelney, and from this base along with the men of that part of Somerset nearest to it, kept up the struggle against the Danes. Then in the seventh week after Easter he rode to Ecgbryhtesstan *to the east of Selwood. And all the men of Somerset and Wiltshire and the people of Hampshire to the west of Southampton Water came to meet him there and welcomed him gladly. And next day he left the camp and went to Iley Oak and the day after to Edington, and there fought against the entire Danish army and put it to flight, and rode after it as far as Chippenham, and laid siege there a fortnight. Then the Danes gave him preliminary hostages and solemn oaths that they would leave his kingdom, and also promised him that their king would receive baptism; and they kept their promise. And three weeks later Guthrum, their King came to him, along with thirty of their most esteemed men, at Aller, which is near Athelney, and there Alfred stood sponsor for him at baptism; and the ceremonial removal of his baptismal garments took place at Wedmore. For twelve nights he was with the king who greatly honoured him and his companions with riches . . .*

After this, Wessex enjoyed a period of relative peace. A new Danish fighting force assembled but soon sailed to the land of the Franks, while most of the Danes who had been defeated under Guthrum settled in East Anglia. By now the whole of eastern England between the rivers Thames and Tees had been occupied by the invaders. This area of Scandinavian influence later became known as the *Danelaw*. But in 892 the Danes returned and resumed their campaign in alliance with the Northumbrian and East Anglian Danes.

895   In the same year the aforementioned Danish army built a fort by the river Lea, twenty miles above London. Then later that summer a large body of the garrison and others went to the Danish fort, and were there put to flight and four kings' thanes were killed. Then the following autumn the king camped in the neighbourhood of the fort while the corn was being reaped, so that the Danes could not interfere with the harvest. One day the king rode up along the river to see where it could be blocked to prevent them from bringing out their ships. And this is what the English did: they built two forts, one on each side of the river. When they had just encamped and begun the work, the Danish forces realised that they would not be able to bring their ships out. So they abandoned them, and went over land until they arrived at Bridgnorth on the river Severn, and there built a fort. Then the Saxon levies rode west after the Danish army, and the Londoners fetched the ships and broke up all those they could not take away and brought into London those which were serviceable. The Danes had left their womenfolk safe in East Anglia before they left the fort. Then they remained at Bridgnorth for the winter.

896   Then the following summer the Danish army dispersed, some to East Anglia, some to Northumbria. And those who were without supplies got themselves ships there and sailed south across the sea to the river Seine. The Danish army had not, by God's grace, absolutely and utterly crushed the English people, but they were much more afflicted in those three years by murrain and plague, most of all in that many of the best of the king's servants in the land died in those three years. There was Swithwulf, bishop of Rochester, and Ceolmund, ealdorman in Kent, and Beorhtwulf, ealdorman in Essex, and Wulfred, ealdorman in Hampshire, and Ealhheard, bishop at Dorchester, and Eadwulf, king's thane in

Sussex, and Beornwulf, reeve in Winchester, and Ecgwulf, keeper of the king's horse, and many others as well, though I have named the most distinguished.

This same year the Danish forces in East Anglia and Northumbria oppressed Wessex very much along the south coast with raiding armies, most of all with the warships which they had built many years before. Then King Alfred ordered warships to be built to oppose the ships of the Danes. They were almost twice as long as those of the Danes, some with sixty oars and some more. They were faster, steadier and higher than the others, and were built neither on the Frisian model nor the Danish, but as it seemed to himself that they could be most useful. Then on one occasion that same year six ships came to the Isle of Wight and caused a lot of trouble there, both in Devon and nearly everywhere along the coast. The king ordered nine of the new ships to go out, and they blocked the entrance of the harbour to prevent the others escaping to sea. Then the Danes put out with three ships against them, and three more ships were beached on dry land further away from the harbour entrance, their crews having gone off inland. Then the Saxons seized two of the three ships at the harbour mouth and killed the men. The other escaped, but in that one too, all but five had been slain. These escaped because the ships of the others had run aground, and very awkwardly, for three were aground on the side of the deep water where the Danish ships were beached, whereas the other six were all on the opposite side, so that none could reach the others. But when the water had ebbed many furlongs from the ships, the Danes went from their three ships to the three which were stranded on their side, and there they fought. There Lucomon, the king's reeve, was killed, and Wulfheard the Frisian, and Æthelferth the king's companion, altogether 62 Frisians and English and 120 Danes. But then the tide came to the Danish ships first, before the Christians could shove theirs off, and therefore they rowed away to sea. But they were so badly crippled that they could not row past Sussex, and the sea threw two of them ashore there. And the men were taken to the king at Winchester and there he ordered them to be hanged. And those who were in the other ship reached East Anglia very badly wounded. This same summer no less than twenty ships perished with all hands along the south coast...

899 In this year Alfred, son of Æthelwulf, died six days before All Hallows. He was king over all England except the part which was under Danish rule, and reigned for twenty-eight and a half years. And then Edward his son succeeded to the kingdom.

THE BATTLE OF BRUNANBURH

The high point in the ascendancy of Wessex came when King Athelstan, having subjugated the Scandinavian kingdoms of England and ravaged far into Scotland, defeated a combined force of Scots and Norsemen at an unidentified place named *Brunanburh*. The year was 937 and the enemy leaders, Olaf of Dublin and Constantine, King of Scots. Mercians and West Saxons had now settled their differences and fought side by side. The event was so momentous that it was celebrated in the normally matter-of-fact *Chronicle* by a patriotic poem:

937 In this year king Athelstan, lord of men, ring-giver of warriors, with his brother Prince Edmund, won everlasting glory with the edges of swords in battle around Brunanburh. The sons of Edward, with their hammer-forged weapons, split open the shieldwall and hacked at the linden battle-shields. It was natural to them on account of their breeding to protect their land, their treasures and their homes in frequent battle against every hostility. The enemy collapsed, the Scots and Vikings fell doomed....
The men of Wessex pursued the hated people in troops and cut down great numbers of scattering fugitives with their sharp-ground swords. The Mercians

*did not hold back from fierce hand-to-hand fighting
with any of the warriors who with Olaf had invaded this
land across the surging sea in the ship's bosom to meet
their doom. Five young kings lay dead on the battlefield,
put to sleep by swords, as well as seven of Olaf's chief-
tains and a countless army of pirates and Scots ...*

*They left behind the dark-coated, horn-beaked raven
and that greedy battle-hawk, the white-tailed eagle with
its dun plumage, and that grey beast, the forest wolf, to
fight over the corpses and enjoy the carrion. Never
before in this island, as the books of ancient scholars tell
us, was there greater slaughter of men by the sword since
the Angles and Saxons landed here from across the
broad ocean, the proud war-smiths who invaded Britain
and overcame the Welsh, glory-seeking warriors who
established the kingdom.*

THE BATTLE OF MALDON

Brunanburh is told in conventional, generalised terms and
therefore explains very little about actual fighting methods
and the deployment of troops in the field. An impression of
this is given in a vivid and somewhat idealised poem about a
less important battle at Maldon, in Essex, in 991. It deals
with the brave stand made by Byrhtnoth, Earl of Essex,
against a Norse pirate band which had encamped on the
island of Northey in the estuary of the river Blackwater. It
shows that in the year when it was first decided to pay
tribute-money to the Vikings, men were still capable of outstanding deeds of heroism and loyalty. The poem, which is
incomplete, begins with Byrhtnoth's command to his men to
drive their horses far away, a sign that their intention was to
stand fast and never think of flight. Then he proceeds to
draw up the East Saxon battle array on the bank of the
mainland opposite the Vikings:

*Then Byrhtnoth arrayed the warriors there; he rode
about and gave advice, and showed the soldiers how to*

stand and hold their ground, and told them to grasp their shields correctly with a firm grip and to have no fear. When he had set the army in order he dismounted amongst the men whom he loved most, where he knew his most devoted retainers were.

Then a Viking messenger stood on the bank and harshly called out the following words, delivered the threatening ultimatum of the pirates to the earl as he stood on the shore: 'Brave seafarers have sent me to you, and have ordered me to say that you must quickly send precious things to secure your safety. It is better for you to buy off this attack with tribute than to join in such bitter conflict. We need not slaughter each other if you do what we ask, and with the gold we will establish a truce. If you, the commander here, decide you wish to ransom your people by giving the seamen what they have asked, money in exchange for goodwill, and accept our peaceful proposal, we will go to our ships with the tribute money and keep peace with you.'

Byrhtnoth spoke, he raised his shield and brandished his slender spear, angry and resolute he replied: 'Do you hear, seaman, what this army says to that? They will give you tribute in the form of spears, deadly weapons and ancestral swords, war-gear which will be of little use to you in battle. Herald of pirates, take back this reply, give to your people a much fiercer message, that here stands a noble earl with his troop, who will defend this country, the people and the land of King Æthelred, my lord. It will be the heathen who die in battle. It seems too shameful to me that you should unopposed take our money to your ships now that you have come so far into our land. You shall not get treasure so easily. Point and blade must first decide between us, the grim game of war, before we pay tribute.'

He ordered the warriors to hold up their shields and advance until they all stood on the river bank. Because of the tide neither side could get to the other. After the ebb the water came flowing, the tidal streams joined. It seemed a long time before they could launch their *spears. There they lined the banks of the Blackwater in proud array, the front rank of the East Saxons and the ship-army. Neither could do the other any harm except where a flying arrow took a life.*

The tide went out, the Vikings stood ready, great numbers of them, eager for the fight. Then Byrhtnoth ordered a battle-hardened warrior called Wulfstan, son of Ceola, fearless like all his family, to guard the causeway [which joined the island and the mainland at low tide], who with his spear struck down the first man who advanced very bravely on the causeway.

It soon became clear to the Norsemen that they would not be able to dislodge the East Saxons so long as their only way lay across the narrow causeway. So they began to use cunning, and asked Byrhtnoth to fall back and allow them room to cross. Perhaps encouraged by hopes of a glorious victory in open fight, Byrhtnoth agreed – a move through which the battle was lost.

The slaughter-wolves advanced, caring nothing for the water, the troops of Vikings came west across the Blackwater carrying their linden shields to the mainland. There Byrhtnoth and his men stood ready against the enemy. He ordered them to make a shield-hedge with their bucklers, that the line should hold firm against the foe. Then the fight was near at hand, glory in battle; the time had come for the doomed men to fall there. A war-cry was raised; ravens circled and the eagle eager for carrion; there was uproar upon earth. They let fly from their hands file-hard spears, sharp-ground darts; bows were busy and shields were stuck with arrows. The rush of battle was tremendous, and men fell on both sides . . .

A warlike Norseman raised his weapon and protecting himself with his shield advanced upon Byrhtnoth. Just as resolutely the earl made for him, each one intent on evil to the other. Then the seaman threw a southern-made spear which wounded the warriors' lord. He thrust down with his shield so that the shaft broke and the shattered spear sprang out. He was enraged and stabbed with his spear the proud Viking who had given him the wound. Being an experienced fighter he made his spear penetrate the man's neck and guided it with his hand, inflicting a fatal wound upon his sudden attacker. Then he quickly stabbed another, so that the mail-coat burst apart, and he was wounded through the interlocked rings with the deadly dart which was stuck in his heart. The earl was so much the happier; he laughed and gave thanks to the Creator for that day's work which the lord had granted him.

One of the warriors then let a dart fly from his hand which went very deep into the noble thane of Æthelred. Beside him stood a young soldier, a mere beginner in battle who, very bravely, pulled the bloody spear from the man. This was young Wulfmær, Wulfstan's son, who made the tempered spear fly back. In sank the point, so that on the ground there lay the man who had just fatally pierced his lord. Then an armed man made for the earl, desiring to carry off his rings, his armour and trappings and ornamented sword. Then Byrhtnoth drew his sword from its sheath, broad-bladed and gleaming, and struck at his enemy's mailcoat. Very quickly one of the seamen prevented him by crippling the earl's arm. The golden hilted sword fell to the ground; he could not keep hold of it nor use any weapon.

So Byrhtnoth was cut down with the men who stood beside him. But not everyone was loyal and brave for the cowards soon made off for the security of the forest, led by Godric who leaped on to Byrhtnoth's horse to save his skin. This action brought a special curse from those who remained, for there were many who thought that it was Byrhtnoth himself abandoning the fight, and therefore the army was put into confusion and the shield-array broken.

Many points of interest emerge – Byrhtnoth's use of weapons; the importance of the shield-hedge; the assistance of a Northumbrian hostage living among the East Saxons –

from a poem which is one of the most stirring in Anglo-Saxon literature.

THE BATTLE OF HASTINGS

Anglo-Saxon England came to an end as a result of the military defeat of Harold at Hastings, so it is to the story of the battle that we must turn for an account of the last months. Of the several near-contemporary accounts, none is more enlightening than the Bayeux Tapestry itself, and we can do no better than to turn once again to its vivid scenes for a chronicle of events after 1064. Of course it is biased, but then what other account is not? Its aim was to glorify Duke William and to present Harold as a brave but misguided man who, in accepting the crown of England, was breaking a prior oath to support William's claim. The Tapestry was probably commissioned by Odo, bishop of Bayeux and half-brother of the Conqueror, who fought with William and received large gifts of English land as a reward for his support.

One of the features of the politically unstable reign of Edward the Confessor (1042-66) was the rise of powerful families, particularly that of Godwine, Earl of Wessex, who led the opposition to the Norman influence at court which had resulted from Edward's long exile in Normandy during the reign of Cnut. Harold, son of Godwine, succeeded his father in 1053, and in the following years so distinguished himself that he was offered the crown when Edward died without heir in 1066. The commendation of the kingdom to Harold by the dying king seems to have reversed an earlier promise to Duke William, and it is here that the source of the conflict lay.

The first scene of the Tapestry shows Edward in conversation with Harold, presumably giving him instructions to undertake the journey which follows, as a result of which, whether intentionally or not, Harold ended up in France. The travelling party sets off for Harold's estate at Bosham, Sussex, stops to pray and eat, and then embarks upon a sea voyage. It seems unlikely that Harold, a political opponent of the Normans, would have sailed to France intentionally, and it may have been a storm which blew him there. Whatever the case, he lands in the territory of Count Guy of Ponthieu, a vassal of William of Normandy, and is arrested. When he hears the news, Duke William immediately dispatches armed men to escort Harold to him.

After their meeting Harold accompanies William on a military expedition against the count of Brittany. The Norman army sets off in good order, but some of the soldiers become caught in the quicksands around Mont Saint-Michel and Harold bravely rescues them. The party proceeds to the town of Dol, from where it pursues the count of Brittany past Rennes to Dinan. The castle is put to the flame and the count capitulates, handing over the keys of the city on his lance. William rewards Harold with a gift of arms, in accepting which Harold formally becomes William's man. On their return through Bayeux, Harold confirms his obligation by swearing a great oath of allegiance upon the holy relics. Almost half the Tapestry is taken up in reaching this climax, the object of which is clearly to demonstrate William's power and to show Harold as firmly committed to him by formal obligation.

Harold returns to England and visits King Edward. Some telescoping of events then takes place, for the next scenes show the old king on his deathbed, the body prepared for burial, and the funeral procession to Westminster Abbey. The date of Edward's death was 5 January 1066, probably a full year after Harold's return. Harold is offered the crown of England and accepts. When next shown he bears the title *Rex*. Almost immediately a sign of ill omen appears in the form of Halley's Comet, and ghostly invasion ships appear menacingly in the lower margin.

The news is taken to Duke William who straightway gives orders for invasion preparations. Trees are felled, ships built, and a fleet assembled. Arms and provisions are carried aboard and in a panoramic scene the ships carry men and horses across the Channel. The Tapestry makes no mention of any delay in crossing, and the Normans were fortunate in enjoying fair winds at a time when Harold's attention was

Fig 27   The death of Harold on the Bayeux Tapestry

diverted to the north of England because of an invasion by his brother, Tostig, and Harold, king of Norway. After a swift march to Yorkshire he disposed of the invaders in a surprise encounter at Stamford Bridge, but his absence allowed the Normans to land unmolested and his twelve-day return-journey meant that his army arrived at Hastings in a state of fatigue. Instead of Harold's movements, the tapestry shows us Norman soldiers foraging around Hastings, their leaders enjoying a meal, and the construction of an earth-and-timber castle. Both commanders receive reports from their scouts, and the battle begins.

The fighting is necessarily stylised but clearly shows the defensive tactics of the English, relying on foot-soldiers in shieldwall formation, and the combined cavalry, archery and infantry action of the Normans. It is made clear that the Normans met strong resistance and that far into the day the victory could have gone either way. In one memorable scene, Norman horses are shown somersaulting in confusion after stumbling unexpectedly upon rows of sharpened stakes driven into the bed of a stream. In another, William lifts his helmet to scotch rumours that he has been killed. Another scene shows a group of Englishmen isolated on a hillock after the Normans had feigned flight, a tactic they used to advantage at several points in the battle. And we also see the most decisive event of all, the death of the English leaders, Harold's brothers and the king himself. Harold probably did not die by means of an arrow in the eye, as popular tradition has it, but from the sword of a Norman cavalryman, the central figure of a scene labelled 'Here King Harold was killed'. Although some of the English escaped under the cover of darkness, there was no hope for them without a leader, and so, with the death of Harold, the Anglo-Saxon kingdom came to an end.

8

What Survives from Anglo-Saxon England

THERE are many ways in which the Anglo-Saxon settlement has affected the English-speaking world of today, and a number have been touched upon already in the course of this book. The greatest success story has been that of the English language itself, which has shown its resilience and power to adapt, even in circumstances of military defeat, economic change and social upheaval. Even after the Norman Conquest, when French was used in many spheres, the English language was never seriously threatened with extinction. A Browning, Cook, Edwards, Smith, or Webster, living in Barton, Birmingham, Highbury, Sheffield, or Whitchurch, or any other '-ton', '-ham', '-bury', '-field', or '-church', is employing words introduced or adapted by the Anglo-Saxons every time he names himself or his place of residence. Many of the words of everyday English can be traced back to Anglo-Saxon times, and many of the principles by which new words are coined are those of Old English. Not only in the words people use, but in the way they put them together in the patterns of their speech, and perhaps therefore in the patterns of their thoughts, is this direct influence felt.

ADMINISTRATIVE LEGACY

Another area is administration. The origin of the English

counties, and of county division in foreign countries influenced by England, lies in the Anglo-Saxon shire system. Diocesan organisation can be traced back to Theodore of Tarsus, archbishop of Canterbury 668-90. Many of the weights and measures in use today go back to measures introduced by the Anglo-Saxons, or adapted by them from the Romans. The inch, foot, furlong, mile and acre have a long history which, sadly, must terminate with metrication. Pounds, shillings and pence, in the ratio of 240 pence to the pound, were only superseded in 1971.

But, of course, it is in the museums that the most obvious and tangible relics of Anglo-Saxon life are preserved, and in the following pages the best collections are listed and a sample of some of their major treasures described. We finish with a brief look outside the museums at earthworks, stone sculptures and churches.

MUSEUMS WITH INTERESTING ANGLO-SAXON COLLECTIONS

Abingdon Borough Museum, Berkshire
Cambridge University Museum of Archaeology and Ethnology
Canterbury Royal Museum
Durham Cathedral, Dormitory Museum
Huddersfield, Tolson Memorial Museum
Hull, Transport and Archaeological Museum, Mortimer Collection
Jarrow Hall (site museum)
Lincoln City and County Museum
Lindisfarne Priory, Northumberland (site museum)
Liverpool City Museum
London, British Museum
London, Victoria and Albert Museum
Maidstone Museum, Kènt Archaeological Society's Collection
Newcastle University Museum of Antiquities
Oxford, Ashmolean Museum
Sheffield City Museum

Sunderland, Monkwearmouth Station Museum
Weald and Downland Open Air Museum, Singleton, Nr
  Chichester, Sussex.
York Minster
York, The Yorkshire Museum

Celtic material providing a useful background can be seen
in:
Cardiff, The National Museum of Wales
Dublin, The National Museum of Ireland
Edinburgh, The National Museum of Antiquities of
  Scotland

THE SUTTON HOO SHIP-BURIAL

Foremost among the major treasures is the material from
the Sutton Hoo ship-burial in the British Museum. Excavated in 1938-9, this was taken from the largest barrow on a
heathland burial field at Woodbridge, Suffolk (Fig 19). The
funeral deposit, the richest ever to have come to light in
Europe, may be that of Rædwald (d 624/5), king of the East
Angles, although no human remains were identified and it is
possible that no actual body was ever buried.

The objects which suggest a king are an iron stand, 67in
(170cm) high, which may have been a royal standard; a stone
sceptre, 32½in (82cm) long, decorated at each end with carved
faces and painted knobs, surmounted by a bronze stag and
having a bronze knee-cup at the base (Fig 28); and the twenty
or so gold fittings of the harness, which have the appearance
of being official regalia. Also, the unparalleled richness and
craftmanship of all the artefacts make the identification with
royalty very likely.

Besides the stand and sceptre, the main categories are gold
jewellery, silverware, weapons and vessels. Prominent
among the gold objects is a great buckle, over 13cm long,
decorated with interlaced animals picked out in *niello*. All
the other major pieces are set with garnets (over 4,000 of
them) and some, in addition, with chequerwork inlays of

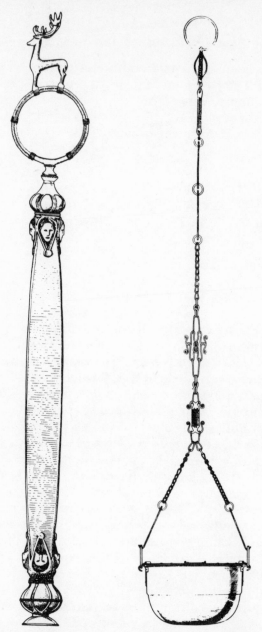

Fig 28 (*left*) Sceptre from Sutton Hoo – 32½in   Fig 29 (*right*)
Sutton Hoo bronze cauldron with reconstructed wrought-iron
suspension chain – 12½ft (*The Sutton Hoo Ship Burial: A Handbook*)

millefiori enamel. Most elaborate is the lid of a purse, 19cm long, its frame containing eleven ornamental plaques and studs which were once sunk into a plate of bone or ivory. The pouch of the purse contained thirty-seven gold coins, minted abroad, three coin blanks and two small gold ingots. There are also a pair of clasps, which had been sewn to the shoulders of some kind of cuirass (Plate 5) and a sword with its elaborate pommel, scabbard-bosses and sword-knot set with garnets. The other fittings consist of more buckles, mounts and strap-ends which were found scattered as if they had once been fixed to a harness hanging from the roof of the burial chamber. The many unparalleled features of the goldwork make the collection of the greatest artistic importance.

In contrast, the sixteen silver pieces form a haphazard collection of only mediocre quality and workmanship. All are from eastern Europe or the Near East and are thought to have been acquired through trade. There is hardly any other antique silver known from pagan Germanic graves.

The largest piece at Sutton Hoo is a dish bearing control stamps of the Byzantine emperor, Anastasius (d 518). There is a drop-handled bowl of classical style and a further set of ten without handles, each inscribed with a cruciform design, which had been buried, inverted, in a pile. A small silver ladle, a silver cup and two spoons, 10in (25cm) long, complete the collection. The spoons are a pair, engraved in Greek letters with the names 'Saul' and 'Paul'. They were probably a baptism gift for a convert such as Rædwald.

The weapons are five spears, three angons, an axe, a garment of chainmail, a shield, a helmet and the jewelled sword already referred to. The last three are almost certainly Swedish. The shield has an ornate iron boss partially covered with gilt-bronze and terminating in a garnet-decorated tip-button. Its curved, circular, wooden orb, now decayed, was about 36in (90cm) in diameter, covered front and back with leather and decorated with a variety of mounts and fittings, of which the most spectacular are a bird of prey and a dragon. The shield was evidently an ancient heirloom when buried, for parts of it had been repaired with plaster covered with gold leaf. The helmet has an iron crown, crest, visor, neckpiece and cheek-guards. The outer surface is covered with sheets of bronze with figure-designs and interlace stamped into them. A face mask incorporates the bronze, silver, garnet and gilt eyebrows, nose and moustache into a flying dragon. A king vested in full trappings, including this magnificent headgear, must have presented the most awe-inspiring appearance.

Apart from those already listed, the vessels comprise: three iron-bound wooden buckets and a fourth resembling a tub 23in (59cm) across; three bronze hanging bowls decorated with enamelled plaques; a pair of drinking horns with rim-mounts and finials of silver gilt; a set of six maplewood bottles decorated at the mouth with silver-gilt; a number of walnut cups with silver-gilt rim fittings; a cup of horn; a wheel-turned pottery bottle; three bronze cauldrons with elaborate suspension gear about 12½ft (3.75m) in length (Fig 29), and a cup-like iron lamp containing beeswax.

The largest hanging bowl has as many as eight decorated escutcheons, one of which, inside at the centre, bears a bronze, enamel-studded fish supported on a pedestal. The bowl was old when buried and had been repaired. There are also remains of a lyre (Fig 10), a pillow, shoes, a bag, combs, a wooden tray, gaming pieces and textiles.

The ship-burial at Sutton Hoo has shaken many established beliefs about the Anglo-Saxons with its vivid exemplification of the vitality and wealth of pagan art. Even the most casual visitor to the collection cannot fail to be impressed and to leave thankful that the sixteenth- or seventeenth-century attempt to rob the grave, noted by the excavators (Fig 19), did not succeed.

THE FRANKS CASKET

This carved whalebone box, 9in (23cm) long, was made in Northumbria about the year 700 and is now in the British Museum. It is named after its donor, Sir Wollaston Franks. The ornamentation executed in a fretwork relief, more lively

Fig 30   Lid of the Franks Casket, showing Egil under attack –
length 9in

than subtle, is based on figural scenes, runes and Roman
letters. The panel on the lid above shows an archer defending a stronghold against attackers. His name is given in
runes as ÆGILI, 'Egil'. He was probably a figure of contemporary legend and may have been the brother of Wayland the
Smith. The designer's objective seems to have been to fill
every available space, and for that reason the figures are
sometimes placed in impossible positions.

The front is illustrated and described in Plate 2. The left
side shows Romulus and Remus suckled by the she-wolf.
The runes around the edge read 'Romulus and Remus, two
brothers: a she-wolf fed them in the city of Rome, far from
their native land'. The back depicts the capture of Jerusalem
by Titus in the year 70. Shown in the centre here is the temple, with the Ark of the Covenant, and in four quarters the
attackers scaling the city walls, the inhabitants fleeing, the
taking of prisoners and a trial scene. Two detached runic
words 'hostage' and 'judgement' refer to these last scenes,
and the part-runic, part-Latin inscription of the border
refers to the other two: 'Here Titus and the Jews fight: here
the inhabitants flee from Jerusalem'. The right side of the
casket in the British Museum is a reproduction of the
original panel, now in Florence. Neither the scene nor the
inscription has been satisfactorily identified – they probably
refer to a Germanic legend whose details have been lost. The
combination of Germanic, classical and Biblical subjects is
typical of the eclecticism of the Northumbrian art of this
period (cf the Ruthwell Cross, Fig 20).

THE ALFRED JEWEL

This is the treasure of the Anglo-Saxon collection in the Ashmolean Museum, Oxford. It consists of a cloisonné enamel figure-design set between a block of polished, rock-crystal and a gold backplate. All this is contained within a gold frame bearing an openwork inscription:

+ AELFRED MEC HEHT GEWYRCAN
'Alfred ordered me to be made'

The narrow end terminates in a gold animal-head whose mouth is a socket made to receive a thin rod, now missing, which was fixed with a gold rivet. The gold is decorated with ribbon and granule filigree, and on the main backplate with an engraved stylised plant.

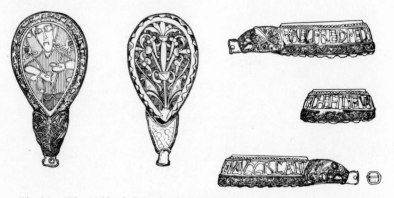

Fig 31 The Alfred Jewel – length 2½in (Ashmolean Museum)

From the inscription, the jewel is usually associated with King Alfred. This is supported by its place of discovery, in 1693, near Athelney in Somerset, where Alfred took refuge at the time of his lowest fortunes in 878, and where he later built a monastery. The function is uncertain, but it is possible that this is part of an *æstel* of the type mentioned by Alfred in the 'Preface' to his translation of *Cura Pastoralis*. In despatching copies of his translation to various monasteries he wrote: 'In each is an *æstel* (? pointer) worth

50 mancuses. And I command in God's name that no one take the *æstel* from the book, nor the book from the minster'. The suggested interpretation of the enigmatic enamelled figure on the jewel as a personification of sight (cf the Fuller Brooch, Fig 8) would, if accepted, also support the idea that this was a device to guide the reader's eye.

ST CUTHBERT'S RELICS

The most impressive setting for any collection is the monks' dormitory in Durham Cathedral, which houses the relics of St Cuthbert, a fine collection of carved stones and casts, and a library of manuscripts. Cuthbert died in 687 and was buried next to the altar in the church on Lindisfarne. His reputation for saintliness, which began during his lifetime, grew steadily after his death. In 698 his tomb was opened and the body found to be miraculously 'uncorrupted' after eleven years. The bishop of Lindisfarne ordered the body to be enshrined in a light chest and kept above ground in the sanctuary where it might be properly venerated. This elevation marks the beginning of the cult which was to become as popular as that of St Thomas Becket at Canterbury.

The shrine escaped desecration in the Viking attacks of the eighth and ninth centuries and, although with difficulty, the brethren continued to live beside the bones of their saint, on the spot where the first Celtic Christian monastery in Northumbria had been built. But, in 875, Viking activity made it impossible for the community to remain, and it set off to find another home, taking its most precious relics with it and, in compliance with Cuthbert's dying wish, the body of the saint himself. A home was found for them at Chester-le-Street in 883, but insecurity forced the monks to move on again, late in the tenth century. Eventually they decided to settle at a spot with strong natural defences, Durham, and built there a little timber church, soon replaced by a grander one of stone, and later by the magnificent Norman cathedral which still stands on the spot.

During its history, St Cuthbert's holy shrine has been the subject of much interest, both sympathetic and hostile. The coffin was opened several times for the kings of Wessex, among them Athelstan who, in 934, presented to the shrine vestments, plate, precious manuscripts, jewellery, church furnishings and, with his army, a gift of money amounting to almost 100lb (45kg) of silver. But the commissioners at the Dissolution in 1538 treated the shrine less reverently. According to a work called *The Rites of Durham*:

> *After the spoil of his ornaments and jewels, coming nearer to his body, thinking to have found nothing but dust and bones and finding the chest that he did lie in very strongly bound with iron, then the goldsmith did take a great fore hammer of a smith and did break the said chest open; and when they had opened the chest they found him lying whole, uncorrupt, with his face bare, and his beard as it had been a fortnight's growth ... Then, when the goldsmith did perceive that he had broken one of his legs when he did break up the chest, he was very sorry for it. ...*

What could be salvaged after the commissioners had finished was afterwards replaced in the shrine by the monks, and was thus discovered in the more scientific investigations of 1827 and 1899. Apart from the skeleton of St Cuthbert and the bones of many others, including possibly the head of Oswald, king and saint, the relics which then came to light are displayed in the museum.

They comprise fragments of an oaken coffin, carved on the outside, probably the 'light chest' of 698. The lid shows the figure of Christ surrounded by symbols of the four evangelists whose names are inscribed in Roman and runic letters – the man symbol of Matthew, the lion of Mark, the bull of Luke and the eagle of John. A pectoral cross of gold and garnets, a small portable altar of wood (later encased in silver) and an ivory comb were probably Cuthbert's personal possessions. The embroideries and braids are tenth-century work and probably all that remains of Athelstan's lavish gift. At least one of the other textiles is likely to be contemporary with Cuthbert, but the fragments are too damaged for their history to be properly reconstructed. Altogether the relics from St Cuthbert's tomb form a breathtaking display in the most glorious of surroundings.

MANUSCRIPTS

Decorated and undecorated manuscripts containing Old English number about 450, but less than 100 have anything more than the briefest notes and records in the language. The earliest are glossaries from the eighth century. Earlier works than this survive only in later manuscripts. Most Anglo-Saxon books are not in Old English but in Latin, and the majority of the richly decorated manuscripts made for church use are of this sort though some of these are older, for example from the Northumbrian 'Golden Age' in the seventh century.

The main types of decoration are miniatures, pages of patterns, borders and frames, embellished text and line-drawings. The most common subjects of the earliest miniatures were the evangelists and their symbols, but by the end of the period a wider variety of scenes and figures came to be portrayed. Patterned pages are found on the earliest manuscripts and make use of ribbon and animal interlace, spirals, chequerwork, carpet-pattern and cruciform shapes. *The Lindisfarne Gospels* is the best known of these. Sometimes these designs were employed within frames to enclose canon tables – concordances of parallel passages in the Gospels. Embellishment of the text took many forms, such as outlining in red dots and colouring-in the loops of the letters. Decorative initials, such as that of Fig 23, were added by an artist in spaces left by the scribe. Line-drawings became a speciality of Anglo-Saxon artists after the middle of the tenth century. They were of two types: either a delicate and sensitive rendering of static subjects like the Crucifixion, or impressionistic interpretations of action-packed scenes such as illustrations to the Psalms.

Manuscripts are subject to many sorts of damage, but

Fig 32   Benedictional of St Æthelwold, made at Winchester
c 980: the Ascension (J. H. Middleton, *Illuminated Manuscripts in
Classical and Medieval Times*)

perhaps the greatest and most wanton harm was done at the
Dissolution, and particularly after Edward VI's 1550 Act
against Superstitious Books and Images. Muniments, service
books and libraries of Anglo-Saxon and later date were
thoughtlessly burned and scattered.

Later, antiquaries began to collect the remnants. Men like
Sir Robert Cotton (1571-1631), whose family had grown rich
from the proceeds of the dissolved monasteries, built up
whole libraries of such books. Cotton's own contained
manuscripts of most versions of the *Anglo-Saxon Chronicle*,
the unique manuscript of Asser's *Life of King Alfred*, the
oldest manuscript of Bede's *Ecclesiastical History*, the best
manuscripts of Anglo-Saxon laws, Orosius' *History*,

Gregory's *Cura Pastoralis*, Ælfric's *Homilies*, *The Lindisfarne Gospels*, *Beowulf*, and so on. After Cotton's death his library was partially destroyed by fire, the *Beowulf* manuscript being one of those which sustained damage. The collection is now in the British Library, where the volumes bear the names of the emperors under whose busts they were shelved in Cotton's day. *Beowulf*, for instance, is Vitellius A XV.

The libraries richest in Anglo-Saxon manuscripts are: the British Library; the Bodleian Library, Oxford; Cambridge University Library, and the Library of Corpus Christi College, Cambridge. Specific treasure can be seen at Trinity College, Dublin (the earliest Anglo-Irish illuminated manuscript called *The Book of Durrow* as well as the Irish *Book of Kells*); Lichfield Cathedral *(Gospels of St Chad)*; Durham Cathedral (early decorated Gospels and Commentary on the Psalms); Exeter Cathedral *(The Exeter Book)*, and Stonyhurst College, Lancashire (The Gospel of St John, said to have been taken from the coffin of St Cuthbert, one of the few books still in its original binding).

THE BAYEUX TAPESTRY

This has already been extensively referred to. Evidence of English origin lies in the language of the inscriptions, the use of Ð (capital of ð), the iconography, particularly of the borders, and the general style, which can be most clearly paralleled in English illustrated manuscripts. It is now housed in a special gallery at 6 Rue Lambert Leforestier, 14400, Bayeux, Normandy, where literature and slides can be obtained.

EARTHWORKS

These consist of defensive and boundary ditches, some of great length, and the fortifications of towns and strongholds. The best known is Offa's Dyke, which can still be traced from the Dee estuary near Prestatyn to the Severn estuary near Chepstow. Its instigator was King Offa, who conceived of this great engineering feat in order to define the boundary between his kingdom and that of the Welsh, and so consolidate his territory at the greatest point of Mercian expansion in the eighth century. The Dyke consists of a high bank with a substantial ditch on its western side. There is a footpath for forty miles along some of its most rugged stretches. In the northern part of its course, as far as Shropshire, running parallel to it on the eastern side, is another linear earthwork known as Wat's Dyke. This antedates Offa's Dyke by perhaps half a century and seems to represent an earlier attempt by the Mercians to mark their boundary with Wales.

Another is Wansdyke, which runs intermittently from near Bristol across Avon and Wiltshire to finish near Marlborough. It is actually made up of two separate earthworks, the eastern probably of the sixth century and the western of the seventh. Its northern-facing rampart and ditch seem to have served the people of Wessex as both territorial boundary and defensible frontier. The Wiltshire stretch is the more impressive today.

A different purpose seems to have been served by a series of earthworks in Cambridgeshire, two of which, the Fleam and the Devil's Dykes, are still of substantial proportions. They cut directly across the Icknield Way and face south-west. It is conjectured that they were set up by Anglo-Saxons who had been forced to retreat from the Thames valley into the Fens at some time during their early struggles with the Britons.

Many of the fortified boroughs have grown into large modern towns, which in the course of their history have swallowed up the early defences. But, where large-scale urban development has not taken place, their size and shape can often be seen, as at Porchester, where a Roman Saxon-Shore fort formed the core of a borough which was reinforced by a later walled rampart, cutting off the promontory on which the fort stood. At Lydford, the fine natural defences of a river promontory are supported by a man-made bank still visible across the neck. South Cadbury, a site which legend associates with King Arthur's Camelot, was re-used as a strongpoint in late Saxon times when the innermost rampart of the Iron-Age hillfort was built up and faced with a wall 4ft (1.2m) thick. For sites without existing or natural protection the norm seems to have been a specially made rectangular earthwork of a type still clearly seen at Cricklade (Wiltshire), Wallingford (Berkshire) and Wareham.

CROSSES AND SCULPTURED STONES

Crosses (see p 96), grave slabs, architectural carvings and a multitude of fragments, great and small, are found in many areas of England, but their distribution is uneven, as shown by the following approximate totals of known specimens: Yorkshire 500; County Durham 210; Northumberland 135; Cumberland 115; Lincolnshire 90; Cheshire 60; Derbyshire 55; Northamptonshire 50; other counties below 50.[1]

Some of the most interesting and impressive sculptured stones are at: Bakewell (Derbys) cross and numerous fragments; Bewcastle (Cumb) cross; Bibury (Glos) carved slab; Bishop Auckland, St Andrew (Co Durham) cross; Bradford-on-Avon (Wilts) angels above chancel arch and large slab; Breedon-on-the-Hill (Leics) reliefs and fragments; Bristol Cathedral, slab; Britford (Wilts) arch jambs; Brompton nr Northallerton (N Yorks) 'hogback' grave-covers; Castor (Northants) panel; Chichester (Sussex) reliefs, possibly Norman; Codford-St-Peter (Wilts) cross; Eyam (Derbys) cross; Fletton (Cambs) friezes; Gosforth (Cumb) cross and 'fishing' stone; Hexham (Northumb) cross, 'frith stool' and numerous fragments; Heysham (Lancs) hogback and graves carved into solid rock; Ilkley (W Yorks) crosses; Irton (Cumb) cross; Jarrow (Tyne and Wear) dedication stone, baluster shafts and fragments in porch; Kirkby Stephen (Cumb) cross; Kirkdale (N Yorks) sun-dial; Langford (Oxon) reliefs; Leeds Parish Church, cross; London, St Pauls, graveslab (now in Guildhall Museum);

---

[1] Figures, kindly supplied by Professor Rosemary Cramp and Mr Richard Bailey, relate to the old county boundaries. Further fragments are being discovered as research continues.

Fig 33   Sculptured stone slab at Wirksworth, probably eighth-century – length 5ft

Melbury Bubb (Dorset) font; Monkwearmouth (Tyne and Wear) arch jambs, balusters, grave-slab and numerous fragments; Otley (W Yorks) cross; Orpington (London) sundial; Reculver (Kent) cross fragments (now in Canterbury Cathedral); Romsey (Hants) relief; Ruthwell (Dumfries) cross; Sandbach (Ches) crosses; Wirksworth (Derbys) slab; Wolverhampton (W Midlands) pillar.

CHURCHES

Anglo-Saxon churches rarely survive in anything approaching their early shape. Escomb (Co Durham) has been mentioned as one of the few (p 98), and several others are listed below. But Saxon fabric can often be distinguished amongst later work and the shape of the original church can sometimes be deduced. There are many clues which an architectural historian can look for. Walls are generally thinner than those of Norman churches, and often made of 'throughstones' – single stones running the whole thickness of the wall – where large enough ones were available. These can often be seen where walls are pierced by arches. Walls are often of rubble bound with a strong mortar, or of squared blocks of varying sizes, untidily coursed as if they were to be plastered over.

Large cornerstones, or *quoins*, were set in a number of characteristic styles and often remain visible, deprived of their original strengthening function, where aisles have been added to a nave or when a chancel has been extended. Pilaster strips – projecting stonework resembling Tudor half-timbering – were used to decorate and strengthen some churches south of the Humber.

Fig 34 Type of double window sometimes seen in Anglo-Saxon churches

Doorways, windows and arches are usually very plain, mainly roundheaded, but also pointed or flat-topped. Windows were small, but splayed internally, and sometimes externally as well, while double windows often show one bulging baluster-shaft standing at the middle of the thickness of the wall, supporting adjacent arched lintels on a single throughstone slab. Roofs were steeply pitched (no examples now survive). Towers, usually at the west, but sometimes central, are a feature of later churches and a popular addition to early ones. Frequently they have no fixed stair, and their use is not properly understood. Some churches have crypts, that is, underground depositories for relics, with an ambulatory for the public and a separate entrance for the attendant cleric.

There are over 400 known Anglo-Saxon churches as well

as many doubtful examples. They are most numerous in Norfolk (54), Lincolnshire (47), Kent (36), Sussex (26), Essex (20), Hampshire (17), Northumberland (16), Gloucestershire (15), North Yorkshire (14), Wiltshire (13), Northamptonshire (12), County Durham (11), Suffolk (11), and Surrey (10).[1]

The best, with their most interesting features, are: Barnack (Cambs) tower; Barton-on-Humber (Humberside) see Plate 7; Boarhunt (Hants) whole church; Bradford-on-Avon (Wilts) whole church; Bradwell-on-Sea (Essex) nave of southern-type church; Breamore (Hants) near-complete church and inscriptions; Brixworth (Northants) very large with many points of interest; Broughton (Humberside) tower and stair-turret; Canterbury, St Augustine's Abbey, extensive ruins including three seventh-century churches, tombs of the early archbishops, and monastic buildings; Canterbury, St Martin, part of the first church in England; Deerhurst (Glos) large church and Odda's Chapel; Dover, St Mary, whole church; Earls Barton (Northants) tower; Escomb (Co Durham) whole church; Greensted (Essex) wooden nave unique in England; Hexham (Northumb) Wilfrid's magnificent church with crypt, and also early apse visible through trapdoor in chancel; Heysham (Lancs) ruins of St Patrick's Chapel; Hough-on-the-Hill (Lincs) tower and stair-turret; Jarrow (Tyneside) chancel, formerly separate chapel, and monastic buildings; Kirk Hammerton (N Yorks) early nave, chancel and later tower, now extended; Monkwearmouth (Sunderland) tower; Newton-by-Castleacre (Norfolk) whole church; North Elmham (Norfolk) ruins of cathedral; Reculver (Kent) ruins showing ground-plan; Repton (Derbys) crypt; Ripon Cathedral, crypt; Sompting (Sussex) tower; Stoughton (Sussex) whole church; Wing (Bucks) aisled nave, chancel with crypt beneath; Worth (Sussex) whole church.

1 Based on figures relating to the old county boundaries in H. M. and J. Taylor, *Anglo-Saxon Architecture* (1965).

CONCLUSION

In 1938, Sir Thomas Kendrick wrote about 'the comparative littleness and emptiness of post-Roman archaeology in Britain' and commented sadly that from pagan times 'there is no material that is larger than a bucket or longer than a sword'. Even as his words were appearing in print, work had begun on the mound at Sutton Hoo which was to lead to the uncovering of the great ship-burial. Subsequent discoveries of Anglo-Saxon buildings have been even more useful in their advancement of our understanding of daily life. Archaeology, like other branches of Anglo-Saxon studies, is becoming increasingly technical; but there is still opportunity for the interested and intelligent amateur. Whether he simply goes armed with a placename dictionary as he travels the countryside, or joins one of the expertly led teams of archaeologists who every year investigate Anglo-Saxon sites throughout England,[1] his interest will bring him greater understanding of an industrious and independent-minded people, who, in establishing themselves in a new land, became the first Englishmen.

[1] Details in *Calendar of Excavations*, published by the Council for British Archaeology.

Bibliography

ADDYMAN, P. V. 'The Anglo-Saxon House', in CLEMOES, P., ed. *Anglo-Saxon England*, Vol I (Cambridge, 1972)

ATTENBOROUGH, F. L. *The Laws of the Earliest English Kings* (Cambridge, 1922)

BATTISCOMBE, C. F., ed. *The Relics of St Cuthbert* (Oxford, 1956)

BAUGH, A. C. *A History of the English Language* (1959)

BEDE. *The Ecclesiastical History of the English People.* Numerous translations are available

BLAIR, P. H. *An Introduction to Anglo-Saxon England* (Cambridge, 1959)

BONSER, W. *The Medical Background of Anglo-Saxon England* (1963)

BRITISH MUSEUM. *Guide to Anglo-Saxon Antiquities* (1923)

BROWN, G. BALDWIN. *The Arts in Early England* (1915-37)

BRUCE-MITFORD, R. L. S. *The Sutton Hoo Ship Burial: a Handbook* (1972)

——. *Aspects of Anglo-Saxon Archaeology* (1974)

CAMERON, K. *English Place Names* (1961)

COLGRAVE, B. (trans). *Two Lives of Saint Cuthbert* (Cambridge, 1940)

COLLINGWOOD, W. G. *Northumbrian Crosses of the pre-Norman Age* (1927)

COLVIN, H. M., ed. *The History of the King's Works*, Vol I (1963)

Current Archaeology. Reconstructions of pit-huts in Vols 21 and 40 (1970 and 1974)

DARBY, H. C. *A New Historical Geography of England* (Cambridge, 1973)

DAVIDSON, H. R. E. *The Sword in Anglo-Saxon England* (Oxford, 1962)

——. *Gods and Myths of Northern Europe* (1964)

DOUGLAS, D. C. and GREENWAY, G., ed. *English Historical*

Documents Vol II, 1042-1189 (1953)

EKWALL, E. *The Concise Oxford Dictionary of English Place-Names* (Oxford, 1960)

ENGLISH PLACE-NAME SOCIETY. *Publications* (by county)

FISHER, E. A. *Introduction to Anglo-Saxon Architecture* (1959)

GARMONSWAY, G. N. (trans). *The Anglo-Saxon Chronicle* (1954)

GLOB, P. V. *The Bog People* (1969)

GODFREY, C. J. *The Church in Anglo-Saxon England* (Cambridge, 1962)

GORDON, R. K. (trans). *Anglo-Saxon Poetry* (1954)

GREENFIELD, S. B. *A Critical History of Old English Literature* (1965)

GROHSKOPF, B. *From Age to Age.* Contains partial translation of Ælfric's *Colloquy* (New York, 1968)

HARDEN, D. B., ed. *Dark Age Britain* (1956)

HINTON, D. A. *A Catalogue of the Anglo-Saxon Ornamental Metalwork 700-1100 in the Ashmolean Museum* (Oxford, 1974)

JESSUP, R. *Anglo-Saxon Jewellery* (Aylesbury, 1974)

KENDRICK, T. D. *Anglo-Saxon Art to 900* (1938)

——. *Late Saxon and Viking Art* (1949)

LOYN, H. R. *Anglo-Saxon England and the Norman Conquest* (1962)

MEANEY, A. *A Gazetteer of Early Anglo-Saxon Burial Sites* (1964)

Medieval Archaeology. Journal containing much detailed material

MYRES, J. N. L. *Anglo-Saxon Pottery and the Settlement of England* (Oxford, 1969)

PAGE, R. I. *Life in Anglo-Saxon England* (1970)

——. *An Introduction to English Runes* (1973)

RICKERT, M. *Painting in Britain in the Middle Ages* (1965)

ROBERTSON, A. J. *Anglo-Saxon Charters* (Cambridge, 1956)

ROWLEY, T., ed. *British Archaeological Reports 6: Anglo-Saxon Settlement and Landscape* (Oxford, 1974)

SEEBOHM, M . E. *The Evolution of the English Farm* (1952)

STENTON, F. M., ed. *The Bayeux Tapestry* (1965)

STENTON, F. M. *Anglo-Saxon England.* (Oxford, 1971). Standard work

STORMS, G. *Anglo-Saxon Magic* (The Hague, 1948)

SWANTON, M. *Anglo-Saxon Prose* (1975). Contains good selection of material in translation

TACITUS. *Dialogus, Agricola, Germania* (Loeb, 1946). Text and translation

WELLS, C. *Bones, Bodies and Disease* (1964)

WHITELOCK, D. *Anglo-Saxon Wills* (Cambridge, 1930)

——. *The Beginnings of English Society* (1952)

——., ed. *English Historical Documents Vol I, c 500-1042* (1955)

WILSON, D. M. *Anglo-Saxon Ornamental Metalwork 700-1100 in the British Museum* (1964)

——. *The Anglo-Saxons* (1971)

WRIGHT, D. (trans) *Beowulf* (1957)

I GRATEFULLY acknowledge help received in writing this book from Mr Richard Bailey; Professor N. F. Blake; Professor Rosemary Cramp; Mr J. Hall; Mr Douglas Hamer; Mrs M. U. Jones; Mr K. L. Neal; Professor R. M. Wilson. Drawings not otherwise acknowledged are by the author.

Index

Entries in **bold type** refer to illustrations